The Strange Career of Jim Crow

The Strange Career
of Jim Crow

THIRD REVISED EDITION

C. VANN WOODWARD

New York OXFORD UNIVERSITY PRESS 1974

OXFORD UNIVERSITY PRESS

London   Oxford   New York
Glasgow   Toronto   Melbourne   Wellington
Cape Town   Ibadan   Nairobi   Dar es Salaam   Lusaka   Addis Ababa
Delhi   Bombay   Calcutta   Madras   Karachi   Lahore   Dacca
Kuala Lumpur   Singapore   Hong Kong   Tokyo

Preface to the Third Revised Edition

The previous revision of this book, published in its
original edition nearly twenty years ago, brought the
account up to the events of August 1965. That was a
fateful month in the strange career of segregation and
the movement against it. On 6 August Congress passed
and the President signed the Voting Rights Act, and
on 11 August the terrible riot in Watts initiated four
summers of violent racial explosions all over the country. Thus within one week a historic movement
reached a peak of achievement and optimism and immediately confronted the beginning of a period of
challenge and reaction that called in question some of
its greatest hopes and most important assumptions. To
leave the story at that critical juncture would seem to
shirk an obligation to readers who have lived through
the bewildering changes of subsequent years and seek
an understanding of how they relate to previous developments.

The crux of the problem of relating the more recent developments to those prior to the summer of 1965 is an apparent paradox—the paradox of the most violent revolt coming on the heels of the most encouraging progress in civil rights. The explanation is not a simple one, as we shall see, and many years will probably pass before the problem can be brought into clear perspective and all its aspects properly understood.

In the meantime it would help to recall a certain ambivalence that black people have felt all along toward integration in white America, an old ambivalence that had been buried and put aside during the long struggle against segregation and discrimination. While resenting and opposing compulsory segregation, they had clung at the same time to the desire for enough racial distinctiveness and separateness to enable them to preserve a sense of cultural identity and racial pride and unity. Even the most complete victory over segregation would not satisfy that need, for few wished to deny racial identity or lose it in a white society. The ambivalence created a tension between those leaders of the race who were concerned mainly with protest against racial prejudice, injustice, and segregation and those mainly concerned with the preservation and fostering of racial identity, pride, and autonomy.

Booker T. Washington, who belonged to the latter camp rather than to the former, believed that he could justify an accommodation with white supremacy that would leave the Negro free to build up the black community by self-help and thereby foster race pride and cultural autonomy. Even before his death in 1915, many blacks rejected his compromise. As the Jim Crow system expanded and Negroes were subjected to ever more humiliation, the Washington doctrine of racial pride and voluntary community autonomy seemed more and more hollow and false. It could be seen as an accommodation to compulsory segregation, a submission to white supremacy. New leaders insisted that the goal of racial identity and autonomy would have to give way to the struggle against forcible segregation, that the destruction of the Jim Crow system and the regaining of civil rights had to come first. For the next half-century the black leaders were mainly preoccupied with that struggle, and the idea of a voluntary Negro community virtually disappeared from respectable discussion.

The felt need and legitimate concern for black community remained lodged in the people's minds even though subordinated to the struggle against segregation. By 1965, however, when victory over legal Jim Crow at last seemed almost assured, the suppressed yearning for separate racial identity burst forth with startling force. Its spokesmen accused civil rights leaders of asking that racial identity be forfeited and offering integration as a substitute. But integration with white culture, they declared, was a betrayal of racial identity and an insult to racial pride.

Hence the paradox of victory of the civil rights movement coinciding with violent escalation of protest. The new outburst was protesting something else. Its leaders were to offer some strange programs—all the old varieties of black nationalism, including the back-to-Africa one, and many new ones as well. Some expressions of the impulse were irrational and some were violent, but behind them were genuine needs that the struggle against segregation had not fulfilled.

This revision is confined almost entirely to the addition of a chapter treating events since August 1965. Those readers interested in scholarly disputes over interpretations of the previous history offered in earlier chapters may consult the author's account in 'The Strange Career of a Historical Controversy' in his *American Counterpoint: Slavery and Racism in the North-South Dialogue* (1971).

C. V. W.

New Haven
October 1973

Preface to the Second Revised Edition

The ten years that have passed since the original edition of this book was published have been crowded with unanticipated developments and revolutionary changes at the very center of the subject under consideration. The old edition had begun to suffer under some of the handicaps that might be expected in a history of the American Revolution published in 1776, or a history of the First Reconstruction dated 1865. The intervening years of social upheaval and political travail since 1955 have inevitably altered the perspective from which the earlier history was viewed. They have magnified the significance of some things and diminished the significance once attached to others. They have also stirred deeper emotions, aroused larger expectations, and provoked quicker tempers and shorter tolerance for divergent views than prevailed in discussions of the subject a decade ago.

One purpose of this revised edition is, if possible, to

take advantage of the new perspective the additional years provide without falling prey to distortions that the deeply aroused emotions of those same years have also contributed.

A second purpose of this revision is to add a brief account of the main developments in the history of Jim Crow during the last ten years. Since these have proved to be the most eventful and climactic years in the whole history of the subject, the undertaking is beset with many risks. Not the least of these is the very closeness to events, the immediacy of lived experience, and the lack of perspective which were among the risks assumed in undertaking the original account—and from which it admittedly suffered.

A third purpose of revision is to take into account the many scholarly contributions to the field that have appeared in the intervening years. In the Preface to the first edition I said: 'Since I am therefore dealing with a period of the past that has not been adequately investigated, and also with events of the present that have come too rapidly and recently to have been properly digested and understood, it is rather inevitable that I shall make some mistakes. I shall expect and hope to be corrected.'

These expectations have not proved unwarranted. Historians have been challenged by current interest in the subject to press their researches into many aspects and periods of Negro history that had not previously been investigated. They have in recent years published studies illuminating the history of segregation in slavery and in the ante-bellum North, in Reconstruction and in the period following, in the Populist revolt and the Progressive period, as well as the more recent periods. Many of their findings lend support to my own, some offer criticisms, and some challenge certain interpretations I have advanced. All have served to enrich the discussion. Without exception they have been offered in a spirit of detachment, generosity, and courtesy that I shall try to emulate in making use of their findings and dealing with their criticisms in revising my own work. I have not been able to encompass all the vast outpouring of scholarship, and have had to neglect certain fields, such as constitutional law. I hope that I have adequately acknowledged my obligations to works I have used either in the text or in the 'Notes on Reading.'

Books that deal with subjects over which current political controversy rages are prone to uses and interpretations beyond the author's intentions or control. The present work has proved no exception, and the author has been embarrassed by finding it cited—and misinterpreted—for purposes with which he sympathizes as well as for purposes he deplores. This experience will no doubt be repeated, but the following caveat is nevertheless offered in the hope of forestalling as much misunderstanding as possible.

This study focuses on the history of segregation and does not attempt to treat all types of racial discrimination and injustice. 'Segregation,' as the word is used here, means physical distance, not social distance—physical separation of people for reasons of race. Its opposite is not necessarily 'integration' as the word is currently used, nor 'equality.' Nor does the absence of segregation necessarily imply the absence of other types of injustice or the lack of a caste structure of society. The concept of segregation in connection with race is not an absolute— though it approached that extreme during a period of nearly a half century of American history. Even during the reign of extreme Jim Crow it was not absolute. Before and after that period it was much less so. Since segregation is subject to the whim of individuals and the custom of localities it could and did crop up in all periods and in numerous manifestations.

In treating race relations before and since the period of legally prescribed, rigidly enforced, state-wide Jim Crowism, I am aware that contrary tendencies were always present. Instances of interracial intimacy, frequency of contact, and association could be matched with contemporary experiences of an opposite character. In this as in other human relations, the matter of relative *degree* is important. Like acts of intolerance, discourtesy, and inhumanity, acts of segregation acquire a new significance when they are endowed with the compulsory conformity of 'folkways' or the majesty of the law. There would seem to be no convenient way of measuring the incidence of tolerance, courtesy, and humaneness in a society. Yet the historian may discern between periods significant variation in the prevalence of these virtues. Any variations are important, but they are especially significant when the comparison includes periods characterized by the conspicuous absence of those qualities. It is with these assumptions that periods of race relations and segregation are discussed and compared in the pages that follow.

A preoccupation with legal aspects of segregation in parts of this investigation has misled some readers. I am convinced that law has a special importance in the history of segregation, more importance than some sociologists would allow, and that the emphasis on legal history is justified. At the same time I want to stress that law is not the whole story. Segregation often anticipated and frequently exceeded the law. Sometimes law merely sanctioned what had become erratically practiced by custom. And sometimes reform of the law merely registered the disturbed consciences and pious hopes of remote regional majorities essentially unaffected by the law's demands and not vitally concerned about its enforcement. To make this admission, however, is not to dismiss the importance of law.

Among the shortcomings of this brief study is a neglect of segregation outside the South. I have added a brief treatment of Jim Crowism in the ante-bellum North in the revision because I was able to take advantage of an excellent book on the subject recently published. Unfortunately no comparable study has been published on the North after the Civil War, and my own competence does not extend that far. It is for these reasons and not on the mistaken assumption that Jim Crow disappeared in the North after the Civil War that I have neglected to treat this aspect of the subject and have concentrated on the later rise of the system in the South.

New Haven   C. V. W.
August 1965

Preface to the First Edition

The period of history that gave rise to the laws of segregation, which we call the 'Jim Crow' system, is still wrapped in a good deal of obscurity. For all but the elderly it lies below the threshold of living memory. Yet it is too recent to have received serious investigation from any but a few specialists. Their findings have not made their way into the books read by intelligent laymen, much less into the popular mind.

Southerners and other Americans of middle age or even older are contemporaries of Jim Crow. They grew up along with the system. Unable to remember a time when segregation was not the general rule and practice, they have naturally assumed that things have 'always been that way.' Or if not always, then 'since slavery times,' or 'since The War,' or 'since Reconstruction.' Some even think of the system as existing along with slavery. Few have any idea of the relative recency of the

Jim Crow laws, or any clear notion of how, when, and why the system arose. There is nothing in their history books that gives them much help. And there is considerable in the books that is likely to mislead and confuse them.

It has been my experience that impatient reformers are as surprised or incredulous as foot-dragging conservatives when confronted by some of the little-known history of Jim Crow. The fact seems to be that people of all shades of opinion—radical, liberal, conservative, and reactionary—as well as people of both the Negro and white races have often based their opinions on shaky historical foundations or downright misinformation. Some of the most direful predictions of disaster as well as some of the most hopeful forecasts of interracial felicity have been so founded. And so also have some recent programs of reform as well as stratagems of resistance to reform.

The twilight zone that lies between living memory and written history is one of the favorite breeding places of mythology. This particular twilight zone has been especially prolific in the breeding of legend. The process has been aided by the old prejudices, the deeply stirred emotions, and the sectional animosities that always distort history in any zone, however well illuminated by memory or research.

The distortions and perversions that have taken place in Jim Crow history are all the more regrettable in view of the current debate that rages over segregation. The national discussion over the questions of how deeply

rooted, how ineradicable, and how amenable to change
the segregation practices really are is being conducted
against a background of faulty or inadequate historical
information. And some of the most widely held sociological theories regarding segregation are based upon er-
roneous history.

It is my hope in these pages to turn a few beams of
light into the twilight zone and if possible to light up
a few of its corners. A general illumination will have to
wait upon more research and investigation—work that
very much needs doing. I also make the attempt to relate
the origins and development of Jim Crowism to the bewilderingly rapid changes that have occurred in race relations during the past few years. Since I am therefore
dealing with a period of the past that has not been adequately investigated, and also with events of the present
that have come too rapidly and recently to have been
properly digested and understood, it is rather inevitable
that I shall make some mistakes. I shall expect and hope
to be corrected. In the meantime, I feel that the need of
the times for whatever light the historian has to shed
upon a perplexing and urgent problem justifies this
somewhat premature effort.

These lectures were delivered early in the fall at the
University of Virginia as the James W. Richard Lectures
of 1954. They were given before unsegregated audiences
and they were received in that spirit of tolerance and
open-mindedness that one has a right to expect at a university with such a tradition and such a founder.

February 1955   C. V. W.

Acknowledgments

In the revision of this book I have been aided by the
suggestions and criticisms of many scholars. Among these
I should like to mention especially my obligations to
August Meier, Willie Lee Rose, James M. McPherson,
Louis Harlan, Tilden Edelstein, J. Rogers Hollinsworth,
Dewey Grantham, Jr., and Barrington Parker. My obligation to the work of other historians is indicated at the
end of the book, but I should like to mention particularly two early investigators of this field, George B. Tindall and the late Vernon L. Wharton.

I still feel my indebtedness to four generous friends
who read and criticized the manuscript of the original
edition. They are the late Professor Howard K. Beale,
Manning J. Dauer, John Hope Franklin, and Rupert B.
Vance.

Contents

The Strange Career of Jim Crow

Introduction

The people of the South should be the last Americans to expect indefinite continuity of their institutions and social arrangements. Other Americans have less reason to be prepared for sudden change and lost causes. Apart from Southerners, Americans have enjoyed a historical continuity that is unique among modern peoples. The stream of national history, flowing down from seventeenth-century sources, reaches a fairly level plain in the eighteenth century. There it gathered mightily in volume and span from its tributaries, but it continued to flow like the Mississippi over an even bed between relatively level banks.

Southern history, on the other hand, took a different turn in the nineteenth century. At intervals the even bed gave way under the stream, which sometimes plunged over falls or swirled through rapids. These breaks in the course of Southern history go by the names of slavery and secession, independence and defeat, emancipation and reconstruction, redemption and reunion. Some are more precipitous and dramatic than others. Some result in sheer drops and falls, others in narrows and rapids. The distance between them, and thus the extent of smooth sailing and stability, varies a great deal.

Considerably the longest of the stretches of relative stability between major historic faults over which Southern history flows has been that since the break that goes under several names, among them Redemption,* or the Compromise of 1877. It will doubtless occur to some that in fixing upon this period as the longest I may have overlooked the 'Old South'—the South of the Cotton Kingdom and plantation slavery. But the Old South, so far as the Cotton Kingdom was concerned, was 'old' only by courtesy, or to distinguish it from a 'New South.' Purely on the ground of longevity the Old South did not really last long enough in the larger part of the region to deserve the name 'old.' And in some states it scarcely attained a respectable middle age. By comparison with the Old South, the New South, already well past the three-score-and-ten mark, is very old indeed. There is, in fact, reason for believing that its life span fell somewhat short of the three-score-and-ten years, that its demise may now be recorded, and that the so-called 'New' South should really be regarded as one of the several 'Old' Souths.

Lacking the tradition of historical continuity possessed

---

* 'Redemption' refers to the overthrow of the carpetbaggers and their regime. 'Redeemers' refers to the Southern leaders who accomplished the overthrow.

by their fellow countrymen, more familiar through experience with the shifting fortunes of history, Southerners have less reason to expect the indefinite duration of any set of social institutions. Their own history tells them of a well-established society whose institutions were buttressed by every authority of learning, law, and constitution, supported by the church, the schools, and the press, and cherished devotedly by the people. In spite of all this they know that this old order and its institutions perished quite completely. It was replaced by a new order that had behind it all the authority and confidence of a victorious North, a Constitution newly revised by the victors, and the force of the national army. The social and political changes were inspired by a North that was in a revolutionary mood, temporarily determined to stop at nothing short of a complete and thoroughgoing reformation. Yet this new order disappeared even more swiftly than its predecessor and was in turn replaced by a third, now crumbling before our eyes.

Each successive regime in the South had had its characteristic economic and industrial organization, its system of politics, and its social arrangements. It is difficult to assign priority of importance to any one aspect of a particular regime, for all aspects were parts of a whole and it is hard to imagine one without the other. The peculiarity most often used to distinguish one order from another, however, has been the relation between races, or more particularly the status of the Negro. This is not to contend that the Negro's status has been what one historian has called the 'central theme' or basic determinant of Southern history. There is in fact an impressive amount of evidence indicating that the Negro's status and changes therein have been the product of more impersonal forces. Such forces have been discovered at work behind the conflicts that resulted in the overthrow of slavery, the frustration of the Lincoln and Johnson plan of Restoration, the establishment of Radical Reconstruction, the overthrow of Reconstruction, and the foundation of the new order. In fixing upon the Negro's status and race relations, therefore, I am not advancing a theory of historical causation but adopting common usage in characterizing the successive phases of Southern history.

The phase that began in 1877 was inaugurated by the withdrawal of federal troops from the South, the abandonment of the Negro as a ward of the nation, the giving up of the attempt to guarantee the freedman his civil and political equality, and the acquiescence of the rest of the country in the South's demand that the whole problem be left to the disposition of the dominant Southern white people. What the new status of the Negro would be was not at once apparent, nor were the Southern white people themselves so united on that subject at first as has been generally assumed. The determination of the Negro's 'place' took shape gradually under the influence of economic and political conflicts among divided white people—conflicts that were eventually resolved in part at the expense of the Negro. In the early years of the twentieth century, it was becoming clear that the Negro would be effectively disfranchised throughout the South, that he would be firmly relegated to the lower rungs of the economic ladder, and that neither equality nor aspirations for equality in any department of life were for him.

The public symbols and constant reminders of his inferior position were the segregation statutes, or 'Jim Crow' * laws. They constituted the most elaborate and formal expression of sovereign white opinion upon the subject. In bulk and detail as well as in effectiveness of enforcement the segregation codes were comparable with the black codes of the old regime, though the laxity that mitigated the harshness of the black codes was replaced by a rigidity that was more typical of the segregation code. That code lent the sanction of law to a racial ostracism that extended to churches and schools, to housing and jobs, to eating and drinking. Whether by law or by custom, that ostracism extended to virtually all forms of public transportation, to sports and recreations, to hospitals, orphanages, prisons, and asylums, and ultimately to funeral homes, morgues, and cemeteries.

The new Southern system was regarded as the 'final settlement,' the 'return to sanity,' the 'permanent system.' Few stopped to reflect that previous systems had also been regarded as final, sane, and permanent by their supporters. The illusion of permanency was encouraged by the complacency of a long-critical North, the propaganda of reconciliation, and the resigned compliance of

* The origin of the term 'Jim Crow' applied to Negroes is lost in obscurity. Thomas D. Rice wrote a song and dance called 'Jim Crow' in 1832, and the term had become an adjective by 1838. The first example of 'Jim Crow law' listed by the *Dictionary of American English* is dated 1904. But the expression was used by writers in the 1890's who are quoted on the following pages.

the Negro. The illusion was strengthened further by the passage of several decades during which change was averted or minimized. Year after year spokesmen of the region assured themselves and the world at large that the South had taken its stand, that its position was immovable, that alteration was unthinkable, come what might. As late as 1928 Professor Ulrich B. Phillips described the South as 'a people with a common resolve indomitably maintained—that it shall be and remain a white man's country.' And that conviction, he observed, 'whether expressed with the frenzy of a demagogue or maintained with a patrician's quietude, is the cardinal test of a Southerner and the central theme of Southern history.' Whether it was the 'central theme' or not, both demagogue and patrician continued to express it in varying degrees of frenzy or quietude.

Yet in the face of apparent solidarity of Southern resistance to change, a resistance that continued to receive firm and eloquent expression in some quarters, it has become increasingly plain that another era of change is upon the South and that the changes achieved or demanded are in the very area traditionally held most inviolable to alteration. Not since the First Reconstruction has this area been invaded from so many quarters, with such impatience of established practice and such insistent demand for immediate reform. Beginning earlier, but reaching full momentum only in the decades since the Second World War, the Second Reconstruction shows no signs of having yet run its course or even of having slackened its pace.

It had not one but many sources. Perhaps the most conspicuous was the United States Supreme Court and its succession of dramatic decisions down to 1954. But in addition there were many others, including the pressure and propaganda organizations for civil rights—both Negro and white, Northern and Southern. There were also executive orders of Presidents, acts of Congress, policy decisions of federal agencies, actions by labor unions, professional organizations, churches, corporation executives, and educational leaders. Perhaps the most unusual agencies of radical change were the officers of the army, navy, and air force, acting under orders of both Democratic and Republican administrations. The Second Reconstruction, unlike the old, was not the monopoly of one of the great political parties. Behind these conscious and deliberate agencies of change were such great impersonal forces of history as lay behind emancipation, the First Reconstruction, and Redemption. They included economic revolution, rapid urbanization, and war—war in a somewhat new dimension, called total war.

The Second Reconstruction addressed itself to all the aspects of racial relations that the first one attacked and even some that the First Reconstruction avoided or neglected. These included political, economic, and civil rights. Few sections of the segregation code have escaped attack, for the assault has been leveled at the Jim Crow system in trains, buses, and other common carriers; in housing and working conditions; in restaurants, theaters, and hospitals; in playgrounds, public parks, swimming pools, and organized sports, to mention a few examples.

The attack has also been carried into two areas in which the First Reconstruction radicals made no serious effort: segregation in the armed services and in the public schools.

With no more perspective than we have as yet upon this Second Reconstruction it would be rash to attempt any definitive assessment of its effectiveness, of the motives behind it, or of its importance and meaning in Southern history. It may well be that after a few generations the historians will conclude that, compared with the contemporaneous abandonment of the one-crop system and sharecropping, or the rapid pace of urbanization, automation, and industrialization, the crumbling of the segregation system was of relatively minor historical significance.

What the perspective of years will lend to the meaning of change we cannot know. We can, however, recognize and define the area and extent of change. I shall even be so bold as to maintain that recent changes are of sufficient depth and impact as to define the end of an era of Southern history. Admittedly they do not define an end and a beginning so sharply as the events of 1865 or 1877, though we now know that the dramatic suddenness and extent of the changes wrought by those events have been exaggerated. Granting all that, if the earlier eras of revolutionary change can be compared with waterfalls in the stream bed of Southern history, then we are perhaps justified in speaking of the most recent era as one of rapids—and fairly precipitous rapids at that.

I

Of Old Regimes and Reconstructions

The long experience of slavery in America left its mark on the posterity of both slave and master and influenced relations between them more than a century after the end of the old regime. Slavery was only one of several ways by which the white man has sought to define the Negro's status, his 'place,' and assure his subordination. Exploitation of the Negro by the white man goes back to the beginning of relations between the races in modern times, and so do the injustices and brutalities that accompany exploitation. Along with these practices and in justification and defense of them, were developed the old assumptions of Anglo-Saxon superiority and innate African inferiority, white supremacy and Negro subordination. In so far as segregation is based on these assumptions, therefore, it is based on the old pro-slavery argument and has its remote ideological roots in the slavery period.

1

In most aspects of slavery as practiced in the ante-bellum South, however, segregation would have been an inconvenience and an obstruction to the functioning of the system. The very nature of the institution made separation of the races for the most part impracticable. The mere policing of slaves required that they be kept under more or less constant scrutiny, and so did the exaction of involuntary labor. The supervision, maintenance of order, and physical and medical care of slaves necessitated many contacts and encouraged a degree of intimacy between the races unequaled, and often held distasteful, in other parts of the country. The system imposed its own type of interracial contact, unwelcome as it might be on both sides.

With house servants the old type of intimacy was further enhanced. 'Before and directly after the [Civil] war,' W. E. B. Du Bois has written (with some exaggeration, to be sure), 'when all the best of the Negroes were domestic servants in the best of the white families, there were bonds of intimacy, affection, and sometimes blood relationship, between the races. They lived in the same home, shared in the family life, often attended the same church, and talked and conversed with each other.' It is doubtful, however, that much personal association of this type extended beyond the household servants, and this class constituted a very small proportion of the slaves. The great bulk of the bondsmen, the field hands, shared little but the harsher aspects of contact with white people. There is not much in the record that supports the legend of racial harmony in slavery times, but there is much evidence of contact.

In so far as the Negro's status was fixed by enslavement there was little occasion or need for segregation. But within the slavery regime itself there were Negroes whose status was not established by slavery. These were the few hundred thousand free, or quasi-free, Negroes. It was in the treatment accorded these people that the slave states came nearest to foreshadowing segregation. Denied full rights and privileges of citizens, deprived of equality in the courts, and restricted in their freedom of assembly and freedom of movement, the so-called free Negro shared many of the deprivations of the slave. In addition, measures of ostracism were leveled at members of this class to emphasize their status. Free Negroes tended to concentrate in cities, and the urban slaves were subjected to some of the same measures of ostracism and separation to which their free brothers were prone.

Urban life was a small and untypical aspect of the culture of the Old South, and urban slavery was an even more untypical aspect of the Peculiar Institution. In a history of segregation, however, the urban experience requires special attention. Richard C. Wade in *Slavery in the Cities,* has produced evidence of a rudimentary pattern of segregation in some of the larger cities of the slave states. The pattern was not uniform, and segregation was never complete. It did not always have the force of law, and enforcement was not rigid. But segregation

in some of its modern aspects unmistakably appeared in
ante-bellum Southern cities. Hotels and restaurants were
generally off limits for all Negroes, free or slave, and
Negroes were usually discriminated against in public
conveyances, though the races were mixed in some towns
and Negroes were entirely excluded in others. Hospitals,
jails, and public buildings regularly separated the Negroes when they were accommodated at all. As racially
mixed as New Orleans was, the Opera House confined
Negro patrons to the upper tiers of boxes. Charleston,
Richmond, and Savannah excluded them from certain
public grounds and gardens or limited them to certain
hours.

The very appearance of segregation in the cities, however, was a reaction to an opposite condition of racial
mixing. For in the cities of the slave states the races lived
in closer physical proximity and greater intimacy of contact and association than they did in any other part of
America. 'In every city in Dixie,' writes Wade, 'blacks
and whites lived side by side, sharing the same premises
if not equal facilities and living constantly in each
other's presence.' The typical dwelling of a slave-owning
family was a walled compound shared by both master
and slave families. Neither non-slaveholding whites nor
free Negroes escaped this intimacy, for they were 'sprin-
kled through most parts of town and surrounded by people of both races.' In spite of changes in the ratio of
races which resulted in some racial concentration by
1860, the pattern of residential intermixture prevailed
to the end of slavery—and did not disappear quickly

thereafter. The pattern was the same in all cities. 'In no case did anything like full residential segregation emerge,' concludes Wade. 'Few streets, much less blocks, were solidly black.' Nothing quite comparable existed in Northern cities at that time or since.

The purpose, of course, was the convenience of the masters and the control of the subject race. But the result of this and other conditions of urban living was an overlapping of freedom and bondage that menaced the institution of slavery and promoted a familiarity and association between black and white that challenged caste taboos. The celebrated masked balls and other casual relations between races in New Orleans were popularly attributed to exotic Latin influences. 'Actually,' says Wade, 'what visitors noticed about New Orleans was true of urban life throughout the South.' Every Southern city had its demimonde, and regardless of the law and the pillars of society, the two races on that level foregathered more or less openly in grog shops, mixed balls, and religious meetings. Less visibly there thrived 'a world of greater conviviality and equality.' Under cover of night, 'in this nether world blacks and whites mingled freely, the conventions of slavery were discarded,' and 'not only did the men find fellowship without regard to color in the tippling shops, back rooms, and secluded sheds, but the women of both races joined in.' The police blotters of the period are cluttered with evidence of this, but they bear witness only of the sinners who were caught.

In addition to urban factors of proximity there are

important demographic data that help account for inti-
mate interracial association at various levels. In all the
Southern cities during the four decades prior to 1860
there was a striking imbalance of the sexes in both races.
The significant fact is that the imbalance in one race was
the reverse of that in the other. Among whites, especially
in the cities west of the seaboard states, there was a great
preponderance of men over women, always a phenomenon of rapid urban growth. Among blacks, on the other
hand, there was a great preponderance of women over
men, occasioned by the practice of selling off young
males to the country. Among both races the shortage was
always greatest among young adults. This situation helps
to account for a considerable amount of cohabitation
between white men and Negro women and a growing
population of mulattoes. While the census of 1860 listed
12 per cent of all the colored people in the South as
'mulattoes,' the percentage of them in the cities was
much larger, often three or four times as large.

On balance, then, the urban contribution to racial
segregation in the South would seem to be less impressive than the encouragement that city conditions gave to
interracial contact, familiar association, and intimacy. In
any case, it would be a mistake to place too much emphasis on the urban experience, either as evidence of
segregation or the opposite tendency. For the civilization
of the Old South was overwhelmingly rural, and urban
life was quite untypical of it. Five Southern states did
not have a town with as much as 10,000 population in
1860, and only 7.8 of the total population, and an even

smaller percentage of the Negroes, lived in towns as large
as 4000.

City life proved to be clearly hostile to slavery. It cor-
roded the master's authority, diminished his control, and
blurred the line between freedom and bondage. Slavery
was declining rapidly in vitality and numbers in all the
cities during the last forty years of its existence. While
slaves made up 20 per cent or more of the ten major
slave-holding cities in 1820, they accounted for less than
10 per cent by 1860. By that time they composed less
than 2 per cent of the total slave population. A larger
percentage of the free Negroes lived in cities, but their
number was never great. The proportion of both white
and slave population involved in the urban experience
was therefore quite small. The great mass of both races
was completely untouched by it, and relations between
them were shaped by another environment, to which
segregation had little relevance.

2

Segregation in complete and fully developed form did
grow up contemporaneously with slavery, but not in its
midst. One of the strangest things about the career of
Jim Crow was that the system was born in the North and
reached an advanced age before moving South in force.
Without forgetting evils peculiar to the South, one might
consider Northern conditions with profit.

By 1830 slavery was virtually abolished by one means
or another throughout the North, with only about 3500

Negroes remaining in bondage in the nominally free states. No sectional comparison of race relations should be made without full regard for this difference. The Northern free Negro enjoyed obvious advantages over the Southern slave. His freedom was circumscribed in many ways, as we shall see, but he could not be bought or sold, or separated from his family, or legally made to work without compensation. He was also to some extent free to agitate, organize, and petition to advance his cause and improve his lot.

For all that, the Northern Negro was made painfully and constantly aware that he lived in a society dedicated to the doctrine of white supremacy and Negro inferiority. The major political parties, whatever their position on slavery, vied with each other in their devotion to this doctrine, and extremely few politicians of importance dared question them. Their constituencies firmly believed that the Negroes were incapable of being assimilated politically, socially, or physically into white society. They made sure in numerous ways that the Negro understood his 'place' and that he was severely confined to it. One of these ways was segregation, and with the backing of legal and extra-legal codes, the system permeated all aspects of Negro life in the free states by 1860.

Leon F. Litwack, in his authoritative account, *North of Slavery,* describes the system in full development. 'In virtually every phase of existence,' he writes, 'Negroes found themselves systematically separated from whites. They were either excluded from railway cars, omnibuses, stagecoaches, and steamboats or assigned to special "Jim

Crow" sections; they sat, when permitted, in secluded and remote corners of theaters and lecture halls; they could not enter most hotels, restaurants, and resorts, except as servants; they prayed in "Negro pews" in the white churches, and if partaking of the sacrament of the Lord's Supper, they waited until the whites had been served the bread and wine. Moreover, they were often educated in segregated schools, punished in segregated prisons, nursed in segregated hospitals, and buried in segregated cemeteries.'

In very few instances were Negroes and other opponents of segregation able to make any progress against the system. Railroads in Massachusetts and schools in Boston eliminated Jim Crow before the Civil War. But there and elsewhere Negroes were often segregated in public accommodations and severely segregated in housing. Whites of South Boston boasted in 1847 that 'not a single colored family' lived among them. Boston had her 'Nigger Hill' and her 'New Guinea,' Cincinnati her 'Little Africa,' and New York and Philadelphia their comparable ghettoes—for which Richmond, Charleston, New Orleans, and St. Louis had no counterparts. A Negro leader in Boston observed in 1860 that 'it is five times as hard to get a house in a good location in Boston as in Philadelphia, and it is ten times as difficult for a colored mechanic to get work here as in Charleston.'

Generally speaking, the farther west the Negro went in the free states the harsher he found the proscription and segregation. Indiana, Illinois, and Oregon incorporated in their constitutions provisions restricting the admission of Negroes to their borders, and most states carved from the old Northwest Territory either barred Negroes in some degree or required that they post bond guaranteeing good behavior. Alexis de Tocqueville was amazed at the depth of racial bias he encountered in the North. 'The prejudice of race,' he wrote, 'appears to be stronger in the states that have abolished slavery than in those where it still exists; and nowhere is it so intolerant as in those states where servitude has never been known.'

Racial discrimination in political and civil rights was the rule in the free states and any relaxation the exception. The advance of universal white manhood suffrage in the Jacksonian period had been accompanied by Negro disfranchisement. Only 6 per cent of the Northern Negroes lived in the five states—Massachusetts, New Hampshire, Vermont, Maine, and Rhode Island—that by 1860 permitted them to vote. The Negro's rights were curtailed in the courts as well as at the polls. By custom or by law Negroes were excluded from jury service throughout the North. Only in Massachusetts, and there not until 1855, were they admitted as jurors. Five Western states prohibited Negro testimony in cases where a white man was a party. The ban against Negro jurors, witnesses, and judges, as well as the economic degradation of the race, help to explain the disproportionate numbers of Negroes in Northern prisons and the heavy limitations on the protection of Negro life, liberty, and property.

By the eve of the Civil War the North had sharply defined its position on white supremacy, Negro subordination, and racial segregation. The political party that took control of the federal government at that time was in accord with this position, and Abraham Lincoln as its foremost spokesman was on record with repeated endorsements. He knew the feelings of 'the great mass of white people' on Negroes. 'A universal feeling, whether well or ill-founded, can not be safely disregarded. We can not, then, make them equals.' In 1858 he had elaborated this view. 'I will say then that I am not, nor ever have been in favor of bringing about in any way the social and political equality of the white and black races [applause]—that I am not nor ever have been in favor of making voters or jurors of negroes, nor of qualifying them to hold office, nor to intermarry with white people, and I will say in addition to this that there is a physical difference between the black and white races which I believe will for ever forbid the two races living together on terms of social and political equality. And inasmuch as they cannot so live, while they do remain together there must be the position of superior and inferior, and I as much as any other man am in favor of having the superior position assigned to the white race.'

It is clear that when its victory was complete and the time came, the North was not in the best possible position to instruct the South, either by precedent and example, or by force of conviction, on the implementation of what eventually became one of the professed war aims of the Union cause—racial equality.

3

In the South the traumatic experiences of Civil War, invasion, defeat, emancipation, occupation, and reconstruction had profound and complex—sometimes contradictory—effects on racial relations. The immediate response to the collapse of slavery was often a simultaneous withdrawal of both races from the enforced intimacy and the more burdensome obligations imposed by the old regime on each. Denied the benefits of slavery, whites shook off its responsibilities—excess hands, dependents too old or too ill or too young to work, tenants too poor to pay rent. Freedmen for their part often fled old masters and put behind them old grievances, hatreds, and the scene of old humiliations. One of the most momentous of racial separations was the voluntary withdrawal of the Negroes from the white-dominated Protestant churches, often over white protest, in order to establish and control their own separate religious institutions. In these and other ways the new order added physical distance to social distance between the races.

The separations were not all voluntary. Whites clung unwaveringly to the old doctrine of white supremacy and innate Negro inferiority that had been sustained by the old regime. It still remained to be seen what institutions or laws or customs would be necessary to maintain white control now that slavery was gone. Under slavery, control was best maintained by a large degree of physical contact and association. Under the strange new order the old methods were not always available or applicable, though the contacts and associations they produced did not all disappear at once. To the dominant whites it began to appear that the new order required a certain amount of compulsory separation of the races.

The temporary anarchy that followed the collapse of the old discipline produced a state of mind bordering on hysteria among Southern white people. The first year a great fear of black insurrection and revenge seized many minds, and for a longer time the conviction prevailed that Negroes could not be induced to work without compulsion. Large numbers of temporarily uprooted freedmen roamed the highways, congested in towns and cities, or joined the federal militia. In the presence of these conditions the provisional legislatures established by President Johnson in 1865 adopted the notorious Black Codes. Some of them were intended to establish systems of peonage or apprenticeship resembling slavery. Three states at this time adopted laws that made racial discrimination of various kinds on railroads. Mississippi gave the force of law to practices already adopted by railroads by forbidding 'any freedman, negro, or mulatto to ride in any first-class passenger cars, set apart, or used by and for white persons.' Nothing was said about the mixing of races in second-class cars, and no car was required for exclusive use of Negroes. The Florida legislature went a step further the same year by forbidding whites to use cars set apart for use of Negroes, as well as excluding Negroes from cars reserved for whites, but it did not require the railroads to

provide separate cars for either race, nor did it prohibit
mixing of the races in smoking cars. Texas carried the
development further in 1866 with a law that required all
railroad companies to 'attach to passenger trains one car
for the special accommodation of freedmen.' These
three laws, as well as local ordinances of this character,
were on the books only a short while, however, for they
were either disallowed by military government or repealed by subsequent legislatures. Regardless of the
law, the discriminatory practice of denying Negroes the
use of first-class accommodations nevertheless continued
on many railroads throughout Reconstruction and beyond. Not until the arrival of the full Jim Crow system
much later, however, was the separation of the races required in second-class coaches or universal in first-class
cars.

Other aspects of segregation appeared early and
widely and were sanctioned by Reconstruction authorities. The most conspicuous of these was the segregation
of the public schools. While the law might not provide
for it and individuals might deplore it, segregation of
the schools nevertheless took place promptly and prevailed continuously. There were very few exceptions.
The only notable one was the public schools of New
Orleans, which were thoroughly and successfully integrated until 1877. Attempts elsewhere were probably
restrained by the knowledge that the whites would withdraw if integration were attempted. This in fact did
occur at times when desegregation of colleges and other
institutions was attempted. This situation prevailed

generally throughout major government-supported services and facilities. The law sometimes provided for separate facilities for the races during Reconstruction. But even when this was not the case, and when both races were housed in the same jails, hospitals, or asylums, they were usually quartered in separate cells, floors, or wings. All these practices, legal or extra-legal, had the consent or at least the acquiescence of the Reconstruction governments.

In view of the degree of racial separation developed during Reconstruction, some historians have concluded that the full-blown Jim Crow system sprang up immediately after the end of slavery to take the place of the Peculiar Institution. In a full and interesting study of the Negro in South Carolina entitled *After Slavery*, Joel Williamson finds that while 'slavery necessitated a constant, physical intimacy,' emancipation precipitated an immediate and revolutionary separation of races. 'Well before the end of Reconstruction,' he writes, 'separation had crystalized into a comprehensive pattern which, in its essence, remained unaltered until the middle of the twentieth century.'

The experience of South Carolina may have been exceptional in some respects. But in most parts of the South, including South Carolina, race relations during Reconstruction could not be said to have crystalized or stabilized nor to have become what they later became. There were too many cross currents and contradictions, revolutionary innovations and violent reactions. Racial relations of the old-regime pattern often persisted stub-

bornly into the new order and met head-on with interracial encounters of an entirely new and sometimes
equalitarian type. Freedman and white man might turn
from a back-door encounter of the traditional sort to a
strained man-to-man contact of the awkward new type
within the same day. Black faces continued to appear at
the back door, but they also began to appear in wholly
unprecedented and unexpected places—in the jury box
and on the judge's bench, in council chamber and legislative hall, at the polls and the market place. Neither of
these contrasting types of contact, the old or the new,
was stable or destined to endure for very long, but for a
time old and new rubbed shoulders—and so did black
and white—in a manner that differed significantly from
Jim Crow of the future or slavery of the past.

What happened in North Carolina was a revelation
to conservative whites. 'It is amazing,' wrote Kemp Battle of Raleigh, 'how quietly our people take negro
juries, or rather negroes on juries.' Randolph Shotwell
of Rutherfordton was dismayed on seeing 'long proces-
sions of countrymen entering the village by the various
roads mounted and afoot, whites and blacks marching
together, and in frequent instances arm-in-arm, a sight
to disgust even a decent negro.' It was disturbing even
to native white radicals, as one of them admitted in the
Raleigh *Standard,* to find at times 'the two races now
eat together at the same table, sit together in the same
room, work together, visit and hold debating societies
together.' It is not that such occurrences were typical or

very common, but that they could happen at all that was important.

Southern Negroes responded to news of the Reconstruction Act of March 1867 with numerous demonstrations against incipient Jim Crowism. In New Orleans they demonstrated so vigorously and persistently against the Jim Crow 'Star Cars' established in 1864 that General Phil Sheridan ordered an end to racial discrimination on street cars in May 1867. Similar demonstrations and what would now be called 'sit-ins' brought an end about the same time to segregated street cars in Richmond, Charleston, and other cities. One of the strongest demands of the freedmen upon the new radical state legislatures of 1868 in South Carolina and Mississippi was for civil rights laws that would protect their rights on common carriers and public accommodations. The law makers of those states and others responded with comprehensive anti-discrimination statutes. Their impact was noted in South Carolina in 1868 by Elizabeth H. Botume, a Northern teacher, on a previously segregated river steamer from Charleston to Beaufort. She witnessed 'a decided change' among Negro passengers, previously excluded from the upper deck. 'They were everywhere,' she wrote, 'choosing the best staterooms and best seats at the table. Two prominent colored members of the State Legislature were on board with their families. There were also several well-known Southerners, still uncompromising rebels. It was a curious scene and full of significance.' In North Carolina shortly after the adoption of the Federal Civil Rights Act of 1875 Negroes in various parts of the state successfully tested their rights in railroads, steamboats, hotels, theaters, and other public accommodations. One Negro took the railroad from Raleigh to Savannah and reported no difficulty riding and dining unsegregated. Future Congressman James E. O'Hara, a Negro, successfully integrated a steamer from Greenville to Tarboro.

As a rule, however, Negroes were not aggressive in pressing their rights, even after they were assured them by law and protected in exercising them by the federal presence. It was easier to avoid painful rebuff or insult by refraining from the test of rights. Negroes rarely intruded upon hotels or restaurants where they were unwelcome. Whites often withdrew from desegregated facilities or cut down their patronage. Negro spokesmen constantly reiterated their disavowal of aspirations for what they called 'social equality,' and insisted that they were concerned only for 'public equality,' by which they apparently meant civil and political rights. Actually there is little evidence of racial mixing on social occasions during Reconstruction, though there was much mixing on public occasions, particularly of a political character. Native white Republicans were conscious of their minority status and their desperate need for black support. As one of them wrote the Governor of Alabama, 'we must have men who will mix with the negroes & tell them of their rights. If we don't have such men, we will be defeated.' Such men, native white Alabamians, were found, and they worked with a will across the color line.

It would be wrong to exaggerate the amount of interracial association and intimacy produced during Reconstruction or to misconstrue its character and meaning. If the intimacy of the old regime had its unhappy and painful aspects, so did that of the new order. Unlike the quality of mercy, it was strained. It was also temporary, and it was usually self-conscious. It was a product of contrived circumstances, and neither race had time to become fully accustomed to the change or feel natural in the relationship. Nevertheless, it would be a mistaken effort to equate this period in racial relations with either the old regime of slavery or with the future rule of Jim Crow. It was too exceptional. It is impossible to conceive of innumerable events and interracial experiments and contacts of the 1860's taking place in the 1900's. To attempt that would be to do violence to the nuances of history.

II
Forgotten Alternatives

The Redeemers who overthrew Reconstruction and established 'Home Rule' in the Southern states conducted their campaign in the name of white supremacy. The new rulers did not, however, inaugurate any revolution in the customs and laws governing racial relations. They retained such segregation practices as had grown up during Reconstruction, but showed no disposition to expand or universalize the system. Separation of the races continued to be the rule in churches and schools, in military life and public institutions as it had been before. And as the new governments added what few new public services they built—schools, hospitals, asylums, and the like—they applied existing practices of segregation, sometimes by law and sometimes without. But the new order represented no striking departures in this respect.

After Redemption the old and the new in race relations continued to overlap as they had during Reconstruction. The old heritage of slavery and the new and insecure heritage of legal equality were wholly incompatible as ideas, but each in its own way assured a degree of human contact and association that would pass with the fading of the old heritage and the eventual destruction of the new. Race relations after Redemption were an unstable interlude before the passing of these old and new traditions and the arrival of the Jim Crow code and disfranchisement.

One heritage of the old order that persisted far into the new was the pattern of residential mixture in the older cities and towns. A Northern reporter remarked with puzzlement in 1880 upon 'the proximity and confusion, so to speak, of white and negro houses' in both the countryside and cities of South Carolina. This pattern of 'proximity and confusion' continued for decades in the older parts of the South. Another heritage of the old order that kept physical contact between the races from becoming an issue and an irritant was both psychological and economic. The Negro bred to slavery was typically ignorant and poor and was not given to pressing his rights to such luxuries as hotels, restaurants, and theaters even when he could afford them or was aware of them. So far as his status was concerned, there was little need for Jim Crow laws to establish what the lingering stigma of slavery—in bearing, speech, and manner—made so apparent.

At the same time the more confident, assertive, and ambitious members of the race had not forgotten the

vision of civil rights and equality that Reconstruction
had inspired. Still fresh in their memories was an ex-
hilarating if precarious taste of recognition and power.
The hopes and expectations aroused by these experiences had been dimmed but not extinguished by the
Compromise of 1877. The laws were still on the books,
and the whites had learned some measure of accommodation. Negroes still voted in large numbers, held
numerous elective and appointive offices, and appealed
to the courts with hope for redress of grievances. Under
these circumstances a great deal of variety and inconsistency prevailed in race relations from state to state
and within a state. It was a time of experiment, testing,
and uncertainty—quite different from the time of re-
pression and rigid uniformity that was to come toward
the end of the century. Alternatives were still open and
real choices had to be made.

A thorough study by Charles E. Wynes, *Race Relations in Virginia*, finds that in this state 'the most dis-
tinguishing factor in the complexity of social relations
between the races was that of inconsistency. From 1870
to 1900, there was no generally accepted code of racial
mores.' During those three decades, according to this
study, 'at no time was it the general demand of the white
populace that the Negro be disfranchised and white supremacy be made the law of the land.' Until 1900, when
a law requiring the separation of the races on railroad
cars was adopted by a majority of one vote, 'the Negro
sat where he pleased and among the white passengers on
perhaps a majority of the state's railroads.' There were

exceptions, but 'they became fewer and fewer' toward the end of the period. The same was true of the street cars. In other public accommodations and places of entertainment the black patron often met with rebuff and sometimes eviction, but not always, for 'occasionally the Negro met no segregation when he entered restaurants, bars, waiting rooms, theatres, and other public places of amusement.' There were risks, but no firm policy of exclusion, and this 'led many Negroes to keep trying for acceptance, just as it led at least some whites to accept them.' There were crosscurrents and uncertainties on both sides, but in spite of this there remained a considerable range of flexibility and tolerance in relations between the races in Virginia between 1870 and 1900.

More than a decade was to pass after Redemption before the first Jim Crow law was to appear upon the law books of a Southern state, and more than two decades before the older states of the seaboard were to adopt such laws. There was much segregation and discrimination of an extra-legal sort before the laws were adopted in all the states, but the amount of it differed from one place to another and one time to another, just as it did in Virginia.

The individual experiences and the testimony regarding them presented below are not offered as conclusive evidence or as proof of a prevailing pattern. They are the observations of intelligent men with contrasting backgrounds and origins about a fluid, continually changing, and controversial situation. It would be perfectly possible to cite contemporary experiences and testimony of a contrasting character. To appreciate the significance of the following episodes and experiences one has only to attempt to imagine any of them occurring in any of the states concerned at any time during the first half of the twentieth century. The contrast will be less immediately apparent, and perhaps even lost, to those whose personal experience and memory does not extend back quite so remotely as the 1940's, but they might ask confirmation from their elders.

1

Suspicions of the South's intentions toward the freedmen after the withdrawal of federal troops were naturally rife in the North. In 1878 Colonel Thomas Wentworth Higginson went south to investigate for himself. The report of his findings, published in the *Atlantic Monthly*, is of particular interest in view of the Colonel's background. One of the most militant abolitionists, Higginson had lost some of his zeal, but he had been one of the 'Secret Six' who conspired with John Brown before the Harpers Ferry raid, and during the war he had organized and led a combat regiment of Negro troops. In Virginia, South Carolina, and Florida, the states he visited in 1878, he found 'a condition of outward peace' and wondered immediately if there did not lurk beneath it 'some covert plan for crushing or reënslaving the colored race.' If so, he decided, it would 'show itself in some personal ill usage of the blacks, in the withdrawal of privileges, in legislation endangering their rights.' But, he reported, 'I can assert that, carrying with me the eyes of a tolerably suspicious abolitionist, I saw none of these indications.' He had expected to be affronted by contemptuous or abusive treatment of Negroes. 'During this trip,' however, he wrote, 'I had absolutely no occasion for any such attitude.' Nor was this due to 'any cringing demeanor on the part of the blacks, for they show much more manhood than they once did.' He compared the tolerance and acceptance of the Negro in the South on trains and street cars, at the polls, in the courts and legislatures, in the police force and militia, with attitudes in his native New England and decided that the South came off rather better in the comparison. 'How can we ask more of the States formerly in rebellion,' he demanded, 'than that they should be abreast of New England in granting rights and privileges to the colored race? Yet this is now the case in the three states I name; or at least if they fall behind in some points, they lead at some points.' Six years later, in a review of the situation in the South, Higginson found no reason to change his estimate of 1878.

The year 1879 provides testimony to the point from a foreign observer. Sir George Campbell, a member of Parliament, traveled over a large part of the South, with race relations as the focus of his interest. He was impressed with the freedom of association between whites and blacks, with the frequency and intimacy of personal contact, and with the extent of Negro participation in political affairs. He commented with particular surprise on the equality with which Negroes shared public facilities. He reported some discrimination but remarked that 'the humblest black rides with the proudest white on terms of perfect equality, and without the smallest symptom of malice or dislike on either side. I was, I confess, surprised to see how completely this is the case; even an English Radical is a little taken aback at first.'

In the first year of Redemption a writer who signed himself 'A South Carolinian' in the *Atlantic Monthly* corroborated the observations of the Englishman regarding the Negro's equality of treatment on common carriers, trains, and street cars. 'The Negroes are freely admitted to the theatre in Columbia and to other exhibitions, lectures, etc.,' though the whites avoided sitting with them 'if the hall be not crowded,' he added. 'In Columbia they are also served at the bars, soda water fountains, and ice-cream saloons, but not generally elsewhere.' They were not accepted in hotels and numerous other accommodations.

Twenty years later, in 1897, even though many concessions had by that time been made to racism, a Charleston editor referring to a proposed Jim Crow law for trains could still write: 'We care nothing whatever about Northern or outside opinion in this matter. It is a question for our own decision according to our own ideas of what is right and expedient. And our opinion is that we have no more need for a Jim Crow system this year than we had last year, and a great deal less than we had twenty and thirty years ago.' In his view such a law was 'unnecessary and uncalled for,' and furthermore it would be 'a needless affront to our respectable and well behaved colored people.'

Southern white testimony on the subject has naturally been discounted as propaganda. If only by way of contrast with later views, however, the following editorial from the Richmond *Dispatch*, 13 October 1886, is worth quoting: 'Our State Constitution requires all State officers in their oath of office to declare that they "recognize and accept the civil and political equality of all men." We repeat that nobody here objects to sitting in political conventions with negroes. Nobody here objects to serving on juries with negroes. No lawyer objects to practicing law in court where negro lawyers practice . . . Colored men are allowed to introduce bills into the Virginia Legislature, and in both branches of this body negroes are allowed to sit, as they have a right to sit.' George Washington Cable, the aggressive agitator for the rights of Negroes, protested strongly against discrimination elsewhere, but is authority for the statement made in 1885, that 'In Virginia they may ride exactly as white people do and in the same cars.'

More pertinent, whether typical or not, is the experience of a Negro. In April 1885, T. McCants Stewart set forth from Boston to visit his native state of South Carolina after an absence of ten years. A Negro newspaperman, corresponding editor of the New York *Freeman*, Stewart was conscious of his role as a spokesman and radical champion of his race. 'On leaving Washington, D.C.,' he reported to his paper, 'I put a chip on my

shoulder, and inwardly dared any man to knock it off.'
He found a seat in a car which became so crowded that
several white passengers had to sit on their baggage. 'I
fairly foamed at the mouth,' he wrote, 'imagining that
the conductor would order me into a seat occupied by a
colored lady so as to make room for a white passenger.'
Nothing of the sort happened, however, nor was there
any unpleasantness when Stewart complained of a request from a white Virginian that he shift his baggage
so that the white man could sit beside him. At a stop
twenty-one miles below Petersburg he entered a station
dining room, 'bold as a lion,' he wrote, took a seat at a
table with white people, and was courteously served.
'The whites at the table appeared not to note my presence,' he reported. 'Thus far I had found travelling more
pleasant . . . than in some parts of New England.'
Aboard a steamboat in North Carolina he complained
of a colored waiter who seated him at a separate table,
though in the same dining room with whites. At Wilmington, however, he suffered from no discrimination
in dining arrangements. His treatment in Virginia and
North Carolina, he declared, 'contrasted strongly with
much that I have experienced in dining rooms in the
North.' Another contrast that impressed him was the
ease and frequency with which white people entered
into conversation with him for no other purpose than to
pass the time of day. 'I think the whites of the South,'
he observed, 'are really less afraid to [have] contact with
colored people than the whites of the North.'

Stewart continued his journey southward, rejoicing

that 'Along the Atlantic seaboard from Canada to the Gulf of Mexico—through Delaware, Maryland, Virginia, the Carolinas, Georgia and into Florida, all the old slave States with enormous Negro populations . . . a first-class ticket is good in a first-class coach; and Mr. [Henry W.] Grady would be compelled to ride with a Negro, or, walk.' From Columbia, South Carolina, he wrote: 'I feel about as safe here as in Providence, R.I. I can ride in first-class cars on the railroads and in the streets. I can go into saloons and get refreshments even as in New York. I can stop in and drink a glass of soda and be more politely waited upon than in some parts of New England.' He also found that 'Negroes dine with whites in a railroad saloon' in his native state. He watched a Negro policeman arrest a white man 'under circumstances requiring coolness, prompt decision, and courage'; and in Charleston he witnessed the review of hundreds of Negro troops. 'Indeed,' wrote Stewart, 'the Palmetto State leads the South in some things. May she go on advancing in liberal practices and prospering throughout her borders, and may she be like leaven to the South; like a star unto "The Land of Flowers," leading our blessed section on and on into the way of liberty, justice, equality, truth, and righteousness.'

One significant aspect of Stewart's newspaper reports should be noted. They were written a month after the inauguration of Grover Cleveland and the return of the Democrats to power for the first time in twenty-four years. His paper had opposed Cleveland, and propaganda had been spread among Negro voters that the re-

turn of the Democrats would mean the end of freedmen's rights, if not their liberty. Stewart failed to find
what he was looking for, and after a few weeks cut his
communications short with the comment that he could
find 'nothing spicy or exciting to write.' 'For the life of
[me],' he confessed, 'I can't "raise a row" in these letters.
Things seem (remember I write seem) to move along
as smoothly as in New York or Boston . . . If you
should ask me, "watchman, tell us of the night" . . . I
would say, "The morning light is breaking." '

So far nearly all the evidence presented has come from
the older states of the eastern seaboard. In writing of
slavery under the old regime it is common for historians
to draw distinctions between the treatment of slaves in
the upper and older South and their lot in the lower
South and the newer states. In the former their condition
is generally said to have been better than it was in the
latter. It is worth remarking an analogous distinction in
the treatment of the race in the era of segregation. It is
clear at least that the newer states were inclined to resort
to Jim Crow laws earlier than the older commonwealths
of the seaboard, and there is evidence that segregation
and discrimination became more generally practiced before they became law. Even so, there are a number of indications that segregation and ostracism were not so
harsh and rigid in the early years as they became later.

In his study of conditions in Mississippi, Vernon
Wharton reveals that for some years 'most of the saloons
served whites and Negroes at the same bar. Many of the
restaurants, using separate tables, served both races in

the same room . . . On May 21, 1879, the Negroes of Jackson, after a parade of their fire company, gave a picnic in Hamilton Park. On the night of May 29, "the ladies of the [white] Episcopal Church" used Hamilton Park for a *fete*. After their picnic the Negroes went to Angelo's Hall for a dance. This same hall was used for white dances and parties, and was frequently the gathering place of Democratic conventions . . . Throughout the state common cemeteries, usually in separate portions, held the graves of both whites and Negroes.' Wharton points out, however, that as early as 1890 segregation had closed in and the Negroes were by that date excluded from saloons, restaurants, parks, public halls, and white cemeteries.

At the International Exposition in New Orleans in 1885 Charles Dudley Warner watched with some astonishment as 'white and colored people mingled freely, talking and looking at what was of common interest . . . On "Louisiana Day" in the Exposition the colored citizens,' he reported, 'took their full share of the parade and the honors. Their societies marched with the others, and the races mingled in the grounds in unconscious equality of privileges.' While he was in the city he also saw 'a colored clergyman in his surplice seated in the chancel of the most important white Episcopal church in New Orleans, assisting the service.'

A frequent topic of comment by Northern visitors during the period was the intimacy of contact between the races in the South, an intimacy sometimes admitted to be distasteful to the visitor. Standard topics were the sight of white babies suckled at black breasts, white and colored children playing together, the casual proximity of white and Negro homes in the cities, the camaraderie of maidservant and mistress, employer and employee, customer and clerk, and the usual stories of cohabitation of white men and Negro women. The same sights and stories had once been favorite topics of comment for the carpetbaggers and before them of the abolitionists, both of whom also expressed puzzlement and sometimes revulsion. What the Northern traveler of the 'eighties sometimes took for signs of a new era of race relations was really a heritage of slavery times, or, more elementally, the result of two peoples having lived together intimately for a long time—whatever their formal relations were, whether those of master and slave, exploiter and exploited, or superior and inferior.

It would certainly be preposterous to leave the impression that any evidence I have submitted indicates a golden age of race relations in the period between Redemption and complete segregation. On the contrary, the evidence of race conflict and violence, brutality and exploitation in this very period is overwhelming. It was, after all, in the 'eighties and early 'nineties that lynching attained the most staggering proportions ever reached in the history of that crime. Moreover, the fanatical advocates of racism, whose doctrines of total segregation, disfranchisement, and ostracism eventually triumphed over all opposition and became universal practice in the South, were already at work and already beginning to establish dominance over some phases of

Southern life. Before their triumph was complete, however, there transpired a period of history whose significance has been neglected. Exploitation there was in that period, as in other periods and in other regions, but it did not follow then that the exploited had to be ostracized. Subordination there was also, unmistakable subordination; but it was not yet an accepted corollary that the subordinates had to be totally segregated and needlessly humiliated by a thousand daily reminders of their subordination. Conflict there was, too, violent conflict in which the advantage lay with the strong and the dominant, as always; but conflict of some kind was unavoidable so long as there remained any contact between the races whatever.

The era of stiff conformity and fanatical rigidity that was to come had not yet closed in and shut off all contact between the races, driven the Negroes from all public forums, silenced all white dissenters, put a stop to all rational discussion and exchange of views, and precluded all variety and experiment in types of interracial association. There were still real choices to be made, and alternatives to the course eventually pursued with such single-minded unanimity and unquestioning conformity were still available.

2

Before the South capitulated completely to the doctrines of the extreme racists, three alternative philosophies of race relations were put forward to compete for the re-

gion's adherence and support. One of these, the conservative philosophy, attracted wide support and was tried out
in practice over a considerable period of time. The second approach to the problem, that of the Southern
radicals, received able expression and won numerous
adherents, but the lack of political success on the part of
the radical party of Populism limited the trial by practice of that philosophy to rather inconclusive experiments. The liberal philosophy of race relations, the third
approach, received able and forceful expression, but was
promptly and almost totally rejected and never put to
practice in that period. All three of these alternative
philosophies rejected the doctrines of extreme racism and
all three were indigenously and thoroughly Southern in
origin.

That was true even of the rejected liberal philosophy
of George Washington Cable. For Cable had the right,
as he said, to speak 'as a citizen of an extreme Southern
State, a native of Louisiana, an ex-Confederate soldier,
and a lover of my home, my city, and my State, as well
as of my country.' He felt that he belonged 'peculiarly to
the South,' he said. 'I had shared in every political error
of the "Southerner," and had enjoyed whatever benefits
the old slaveholding civilization had to offer. A resultant
duty bound me to my best conception of the true interest
of the South as a whole—the whole South, white and
black.' His book, *The Silent South,* published in 1885,
was as eloquent, thoroughgoing, and uncompromising a
statement of the liberal position on race as appeared any-
where in the nineteenth century. Cable boldly chal-

lenged the Redeemers' philosophy that the South must have 'honest' government before it could aspire to 'free' government, and maintained that there could be neither free nor honest government without equal rights and protection for all citizens—black as well as white. He extended his demand for equality beyond the political sphere and fought discrimination in employment and the administration of justice. He was an outspoken enemy of segregation and the incipient Jim Crowism of his time.

Quite as liberal and more explicitly insistent on racial equality was Lewis Harvie Blair of Richmond. Like Cable a veteran of the Confederate army, Blair was a member of an old and distinguished Virginia family and a prominent and wealthy businessman. In 1889 he published at Richmond his uncompromising attack on racial segregation and injustice and all the dogmas and prejudices that sustained them. The book was entitled, *The Prosperity of the South Dependent upon the Elevation of the Negro*. More advanced than Radical Reconstruction, it called for an end to segregated schools because they branded 'the stigma of degradation' upon Negro children and taught them 'feelings of abasement and of servile fear.' 'The Negro,' wrote Blair, 'must be allowed free access to all hotels and other places of public entertainment; he must be allowed free admittance to all theatres and other places of public amusement; he must be allowed free entrance to all churches, and in all public and official receptions of the president, governor, mayor, etc.; he must not be excluded by a hostile caste sentiment. In all these things and in all these places he must, unless we wish to clip his hope and crush his self-respect, be treated precisely like the whites, no better, but no worse.' He accompanied these demands by an iconoclastic and derisive attack on the doctrine of white supremacy and Negro inferiority, the plantation myth of slavery, the paternalistic tradition of race relations, the conventional picture of Reconstruction, and the optimistic complacency of the New South school of economics. He concluded with a stern lecture on 'The Duty of the North,' which he urged to clean up its ghettoes and 'clear its skirts of the charge of hypocrisy.'

Neither Blair nor Cable attracted a following in the South. Acceptance of their doctrines had to await the development of urban liberalism, which did not arrive in any force until the second quarter of the twentieth century. Our concern here, therefore, is with the other two schools and particularly with the conservatives.

The conservative position never received so articulate and explicit an expression as Cable and Blair gave the liberal philosophy. The tenets of conservatism have to be derived from fragmentary formulations and from policies pursued. The conservative thought of himself as occupying a position between the doctrinaire Negrophile of the left and the fanatical Negrophobe of the right. On the left were the false friends of the freedman, whose zeal for pushing him ahead of himself, for elevating him beyond his proper station in life, and for placing him in high places he was not prepared to fill had brought about his downfall. They were false friends not only because of an error of judgment but also out of baseness of motive; for they had used their pretended friendship to advance selfish ends of party advantage and private gain. At the opposite pole were the Negrophobe fanatics of the South, who were not satisfied to stop with 'Home Rule' and white government, but would wage aggressive war on the Negro, strip him of basic rights guaranteed him by the Constitution, ostracize him, humiliate him, and rob him of elemental human dignity.

The conservatives reminded the Negro that he had something to lose as well as something to gain and that his Northern champions' exclusive pre-occupation with gains for the Negro had evoked the danger of losing all he had so far gained. The conservative's primary purpose was to conserve. 'The better class of whites,' Wade Hampton told Sir George Campbell, 'certainly want to conserve the negro.' Like other conservatives of the period, the Southern conservatives believed that every properly regulated society had superiors and subordinates, that each class should acknowledge its responsibilities and obligations, and that each should be guaranteed its status and protected in its rights. The conservatives acknowledged that the Negroes belonged in a subordinate role, but denied that subordinates had to be ostracized; they believed that the Negro was inferior, but denied that it followed that inferiors must be segregated or publicly humiliated. Negro degradation was not a necessary corollary of white supremacy in the conservative philosophy.

A blunt and artless statement of the conservative posi-

tion is found in the words of Governor Thomas G.
Jones, leader of the conservative wing of the Democratic
party of Alabama in the 'nineties. 'The Negro race is
under us,' said the Governor. 'He is in our power. We
are his custodians . . . we should extend to him, as far
as possible, all the civil rights that will fit him to be a
decent and self respecting, law-abiding and intelligent
citizen . . . If we do not lift them up, they will drag us
down.'

It was clearly an aristocratic philosophy of paternalism
and *noblesse oblige* that the conservatives preached, and
it was inevitable that the attitude should have acquired
class associations in the mind of both its advocates and its
opponents. When Hampton told Campbell that 'the better class of whites' sought to conserve the Negroes, he
added that 'the lower whites are less favorable.' In 1879
a Columbia, South Carolina, editor (quoted by George
B. Tindall) put the case too strongly, perhaps, but registered a common view. 'The old slave owner . . . feels
no social fear of negro equality,' he wrote. 'He feels no
desire to maltreat and brow-beat and spit upon the colored man. He feels no opposition to the education and
elevation of the black man in the scale of civilized life.'
In the conservative mind distinctions of class sometimes
took priority over distinctions of race. Thus in 1885 a
Charleston paper remarked that, 'It is a great deal pleas-
anter to travel with respectable and well-behaved colored people than with unmannerly and ruffianly white
men.' And twelve years later the same paper said: 'The
common sense and proper arrangement, in our opinion,

is to provide first-class cars for first-class passengers, white
and colored . . . To speak plainly, we need, as everybody knows, separate cars or apartments for rowdy or
drunken white passengers far more than Jim Crow cars
for colored passengers.'

An excessive squeamishness or fussiness about contact
with Negroes was commonly identified as a lower-class
white attitude, while the opposite attitude was as popularly associated with 'the quality.' When some militia-
men of Alabama and Mississippi refused in 1887 to attend a national drill in Washington because Negro
troops were to participate, a Jacksonville, Florida, paper
chided them as having 'dropped a little behind the spirit
of the age.' The editor observed that 'when it comes to
adopting a standard of conduct in relation to the treatment of the color question . . . it is more likely that
the example of the F. F. V.s will prevail over that of
these spirited sons of Alabama and Mississippi. We do
not expect *Fitzhugh Lee* to make a blunder in this connection.' And when the same year Negroes protested the
discriminatory policy adopted by a Florida railroad, an
official of the road replied that the policy 'had to be
shaped to suit the crackers, as the road ran through a
good deal of territory settled by that class.'

Negroes themselves were perfectly well aware of class
differences among whites in this matter of race prejudice.
It was this difference that the Negro Congressman John
R. Lynch of Mississippi had in mind in his speech on the
Civil Rights bill in 1875. 'The opposition to civil rights
in the South,' he said, 'is not so general or intense as a

great many would have the country believe. It is a mistaken idea that all of the white people in the South outside of the republican party are bitterly opposed to this bill.' And he pointed to L. Q. C. Lamar, 'my eloquent and distinguished colleague on the other side of the House' as an example of the 'intelligent legislators and well-bred gentlemen' of the opposition in his state. After listening to a debate in the Virginia Assembly in 1877, J. L. M. Curry recorded in his diary with obvious gratification that 'A negro member said that he and his race relied for the protection of their rights & liberties, not on the "poor white trash" but on the "well-raised" gentlemen.' In 1890, when the demand for Jim Crow legislation was rising, the editor of a Negro periodical in North Carolina wrote: 'The best people of the South do not demand this separate car business'; and again, 'this whole thing is but a pandering to the lower instincts of the worst class of whites in the South.'

When Northern liberals and radicals began to lose interest in the freedmen's cause and federal protection was withdrawn, it was natural that the Negro should turn to the conservatives among upper-class Southerners for allies. While there was a certain amount of fawning Uncle-Tomism among the Negroes, there is little doubt that the prouder of them secretly despised the patronizing pose and self-flattering paternalism of the whites with whom they found refuge. It was no sentimentality for 'Ole Marster' that inspired the freedmen, but the hot breath of cracker fanaticism they felt on the back of their necks.

It would be a mistake to picture the Democratic Redeemers as the first Southern whites to appeal successfully to the Negro voter with the conservative race philosophy. That distinction belongs to the conservative ex-Whig planters of Mississippi, turned Republicans, who took over the party from the radicals and dominated it for several years with Negro support. James L. Alcorn, wealthy planter of the delta, large slaveholder, and almost as much the aristocrat as Wade Hampton or Jefferson Davis, appealed to the Negro with a program of civil rights, legal equality, and public education. The Negro vote plus the ex-Whig support elected Alcorn the first Republican governor of Mississippi, sent him to the Senate for a term, and put another Whig-Republican in the governor's office to succeed Alcorn.

During the electoral crisis of 1876-7 the advisers of Rutherford B. Hayes assured him that 'in almost every Southern State you can find men like Alcorn in Mississippi.' Most of these ex-Whigs of the South had drifted into the Democratic party, after some experiments with the Republicans. The outspoken discontent of the old Whigs with their new party and the acute unhappiness of the Southern Democrats with the policies of the Northern Democrats led Hayes and his advisers to hope that withdrawal of support from the carpetbaggers would leave the old Whigs heirs to the freedmen's votes and encourage them to establish strong conservative Republican movements in the South similar to Alcorn's in Mississippi. High hope for such a political development was one among several reasons that enabled conservative Republicans and Southern Democrats to agree on the Compromise of 1877 that made Hayes President. As it turned out, the Southern ex-Whigs disappointed Hayes, for instead of leading a Republican revolt in the South they went far toward consolidating their control over the Democratic party in that region. To the conservative party, as the Democratic party came to be called in the South, the new leaders brought their Whiggish notions of economics and politics, and along with them their conservative race philosophy.

One tenet of that philosophy was an endorsement and defense of Negro suffrage. In a symposium published in the *North American Review* in 1879, Hampton, Lamar, and Alexander Stephens agreed not only that the disfranchisement of the freedman was impossible, but that even if it were possible the South would not desire it. Hampton had often boasted that he was 'the first white man in the South, after the Civil War, to advocate giving the Negro the franchise' and once declared his belief that 'a large majority of the intelligent and reflecting whites' agreed with him on the subject. In the symposium he declared that 'As the negro becomes more intelligent, he naturally allies himself with the more conservative of the whites.'

The impression often left by cursory histories of the subject is that Negro disfranchisement followed quickly if not immediately upon the overthrow of Reconstruction. It is perfectly true that Negroes were often coerced, defrauded, or intimidated, but they continued to vote in large numbers in most parts of the South for more than two decades after Reconstruction. In the judgment of the abolitionist Higginson, 'The Southern whites accept them precisely as Northern men in cities accept the ignorant Irish vote,—not cheerfully, but with acquiescence in the inevitable; and when the strict color-line is once broken they are just as ready to conciliate the negro as the Northern politician to flatter the Irishman. Any powerful body of voters may be cajoled today and intimidated tomorrow and hated always, but it can never be left out of sight.' As a voter the Negro was both hated and cajoled, both intimidated and courted, but he could never be ignored so long as he voted.

Not only did Negroes continue to vote after Reconstruction, but they continued to hold office as well. Every session of the Virginia General Assembly from 1869 to 1891 contained Negro members. Between 1876 and 1894 North Carolinians elected fifty-two Negroes to the lower house of their state legislature, and between 1878 and 1902 forty-seven Negroes served in the South Carolina General Assembly. In 1890 there were sixteen Negro members of the session of the Louisiana General Assembly which passed the Jim Crow railway bill that led to the case of *Plessy* v. *Ferguson*. Southern states elected ten Negroes to the U. S. House of Representatives after Reconstruction, the same number elected during Reconstruction. Every Congress but one between 1869 and 1901 had at least one Negro member from the South.

The governors of the last two states to emerge from Reconstruction rule were both on record with unqualified pledges to protect the freedmen in the enjoyment of

their rights. The pledges of Governor Hampton of South
Carolina and Governor Francis T. Nicholls of Louisiana
were made not only to the Republican administration
but to the Negro voters of their states. 'After I was recognized as Governor,' wrote Nicholls in his autobiography,
'I set myself earnestly to work to bring about good feeling and confidence between the races . . . I was particularly anxious by kindness and strict justice & im-
partiality to the colored people . . . that they should
feel that they were not proscribed & to this end appointed a number of them to small offices sandwiching
them on Boards between white men while they were
powerless to do harm they were in a position to see &
know everything that was going on.' A white supporter
claimed with obvious exaggeration that Nicholls gave
the Negroes more recognition and offices in the first year
of his administration than the Republicans of Louisiana
had given them in their entire regime.

Hampton went further than Nicholls in his efforts to
conciliate the freedmen, reconcile the races, and attract
Negro voters to the support of his administration. The
title of a Hampton campaign book was *Free Men! Free
Ballots!! Free Schools!!! The Pledges of Gen. Wade
Hampton . . . to the Colored People of South Carolina,
1865-1876*. The computation of a reliable source shows
that Hampton appointed at least eighty-six Negroes to
office during his administration. None of them was appointed to an important state office, but they were
named trial justices, jury commissioners, and members
of county and state commissions. Five months after the

new government took control, the Republican ex-Governor Robert K. Scott told Northern newspapermen that 'Hampton is honestly carrying out the promises he made during the campaign. He has already appointed more colored men to office than were appointed during the first two years that I was Governor.' Negroes were placed on Democratic tickets as candidates for the legislature in several counties, they were admitted to membership in agricultural societies in a few instances, and their militia companies, fire brigades, and other organizations were encouraged to participate in public functions and demonstrations. The governor's policies won praise from Negro and Republican leaders of South Carolina of that period and have convinced George B. Tindall, a careful historian, that Hampton was 'a generous and constructive statesman with regard to race relations.' His policy proved to be a failure as a political solution, for not even Hampton's great prestige could long keep at bay the Negrophobe element of his own party. After he left the state to go to the Senate the opposition grew until it eventually repudiated his conciliatory policies, along with the conservative race philosophy, and ended in all-out aggression against the Negro.

If the Negro's affinity for the conservative whites had its practical motivations of self-interest, so did the conservative interest in the Negro. The tradition of *noblesse oblige* and the flattery of paternalistic impulses do not adequately account for the pains the conservative Redeemers took to conciliate the Negroes and attract their support. The fact was that many of the Whiggish policies of the Redeemers, particularly their subservience to railroads, corporations, and business interests, and their support of financial and monetary doctrines of the Northeast, were highly unpopular in the South—especially among the depressed agricultural white population. Calling themselves Independents, Greenbackers, or Readjusters, these disaffected elements organized in third parties and challenged the control of the conservative Democrats in almost every Southern state shortly after Redemption. They presented a serious threat to conservative control in some states, and in Virginia, where they combined with a wing of the Republican party there, they overthrew the Redeemer government and took over the state. In this situation conservatives were obviously in need of friends, and as the third party grew in other states and threatened to repeat the Virginia tactics, the conservatives naturally sought an understanding with the Negroes.

This understanding or alliance as it worked out in Mississippi under the leadership of Lamar and Senator J. Z. George was known as the 'fusion principle.' This was a working agreement by which the conservatives helped the Negro wing of the Republican party against the white wing in return for Negro assistance to the conservatives in their struggles against dissident whites—Greenbackers or Republicans, who often worked together. In practice, the county Democratic executive committee would agree with Negro leaders upon the number of offices to be held by Negroes. The proportion and type of offices varied, but usually the Negroes were

assigned the less important offices and one of the county's
seats in the state legislature. Sometimes they got considerably more, sometimes less. In addition Lamar and
the rest of the Democratic congressional delegation used
their influence and votes in Washington to secure federal
patronage and office for their Negro friends, patronage
that would not have gone to Democrats in any case and
might have gone to white Republicans. On the motion
of Lamar, for example, Blanche K. Bruce, former Negro
Senator from Mississippi, was unanimously confirmed
as Register of the Treasury. The advantage thus gained
by the conservatives consisted in Negro support in local
politics against the Independent party, made up of dissident whites of both the old parties. Other advantages
lay in keeping the Republicans split, preventing able
white leadership from gaining control, and in being able
to discredit the Republican party as being under Negro
control. Using these tactics, as well as the cruder ones of
fraud and terror, the conservatives weathered the Independent and Greenbacker revolts of the early 'eighties.
Conservatives of other Southern states who were faced
with the same kind of revolt also marshaled the Negro
vote against white discontent, using variations of the
Mississippi tactics.

Seeing the Independent revolt in the South as an opportunity to split the white vote and restore Republican
power in the region, President Chester A. Arthur withdrew his support from the Negro leaders and sought to
place native whites in command. Embitterment of Negro
voters over this and other Republican policies since 1877

led conservative leaders of the Southern Democrats to attempt a concerted drive to attract them away from their traditional party. The Negro voters were therefore courted, flattered, 'mistered,' and honored by Southern white politicians in the 'eighties as never before. With the cordial recommendation of Southern Democrats, President Cleveland appointed several Negroes to office in the South. Senator E. C. Walthall urged the appointment of one in Mississippi, Senator M. C. Butler in South Carolina, and Senator Isham Harris in Tennessee. Congressman Thomas C. Catchings of Mississippi boasted that by the workings of the 'fusion principle' there were 'more colored men holding office in my district alone, through the action of the Democratic party, than there are in the whole North.'

Caught between the 'Lily-White' policy of the Republican party and the blandishments of the Southern Democrats, the Negro became confused and politically apathetic. Republican organizations declined in strength in the South and many state parties ceased to put forth tickets altogether. Despite that, the Negroes did not flock to the opposing party. For one thing they knew from long experience that, for all their kind words and blandishments, the Democrats would resort to force or fraud in a pinch. For another, Negro leaders were beginning to think in economic terms and ask their people what they had in common with their white landlords, creditors, and employers that would justify a political alliance with the conservatives.

3

The conservative philosophy of race relations was not the only alternative to extreme racism and proscription offered to the South and tried out in practice by Southern white people. Another approach was that of the Southern radicals, as worked out and expressed by the Populists. The agrarian forerunners of the Populists—the Readjusters, Independents, and Greenbackers—also attempted to reach an understanding with the Negro, but they approached him through his Republican leaders to seek a pragmatic alliance of mutual political convenience. They rarely approached him directly and did not seek to convert him personally to their cause. The Populists eventually resorted in large measure to the same tactics. But first they went over the heads of the established leaders, largely Republican, and sought to convert the Negroes themselves, make them good Populists by conviction, fire them with the zeal they themselves felt for the common cause, integrate them thoroughly with the party, and give them a sense of belonging and tangible evidence that they did belong.

The Populists steered clear of the patronizing approach that both the radical Republicans and the conservative Democrats took toward the freedmen. They neither pictured themselves as the keepers of the liberal conscience and the Negro as the ward of the nation, as did the Republican radicals, nor did they assume the pose of *noblesse oblige* and regard the Negro as an object of paternalistic protection as did the Southern conservatives. The Populists fancied themselves as exponents of a new realism on race, free from the delusions of doctrinaire and sentimental liberalism on the one hand, and the illusions of romantic paternalism on the other. There was in the Populist approach to the Negro a limited type of equalitarianism quite different from that preached by the radical Republicans and wholly absent from the conservative approach. This was an equalitarianism of want and poverty, the kinship of a common grievance and a common oppressor. As a Texas Populist expressed the new equalitarianism, 'They are in the ditch just like we are.'

Dismissing irrational motives as of no great account, the Populists grounded their 'realism' on the doctrine that 'self-interest always controls'—the dubious postulate on which much economic and political thought of their day was based. As Tom Watson, foremost leader of Southern Populism, framed the credo: 'Gratitude may fail; so may sympathy, and friendship, and generosity, and patriotism, but, in the long run, self-interest always controls. Let it once appear plainly that it is to the interest of a colored man to vote with the white man and he will do it . . . The People's party will settle the race question. First, by enacting the Australian ballot system. Second, by offering to white and black a rallying point which is free from the odium of former discords and strifes. Third, by presenting a platform immensely beneficial to both races and injurious to neither. Fourth, by making it to the interest of both races to act together for the success of the platform.'

Deprecate emotional and irrational factors of prejudice as they did, the Populist strategists were perfectly aware that these factors were the most serious of all obstacles to their success in the South. It was even more difficult for them than for the conservatives to defy and circumvent race prejudice, since it ran highest and strongest among the very white elements to which the Populist appeal was especially addressed—the depressed lower economic classes. They were the classes from whose phobias and fanaticisms the conservatives offered to protect the Negro. To master these deep-rooted phobias and create a community of feeling and interest in which the two races could combine required greater political genius than the conservatives had to muster for their program. The wonder is not that the Populists eventually failed but that they made as much headway as they did against the overwhelming odds they faced.

The measures they took were sometimes drastic and, for the times, even heroic. At a time when Georgia led all the states in lynchings Watson announced that it was the object of his party to 'make lynch law odious to the people.' And in 1896 the Populist platform of Georgia contained a plank denouncing lynch law. In the campaign of 1892 a Negro Populist who had made sixty-three speeches for Watson was threatened with lynching and fled to him for protection. Two thousand armed white farmers, some of whom rode all night, responded to Watson's call for aid and remained on guard for two nights at his home to avert the threat of violence.

Addressing himself directly to the problem of color prejudice, Watson told the two races: 'You are made to hate each other because upon that hatred is rested the keystone of the arch of financial despotism which enslaves you both. You are deceived and blinded that you may not see how this race antagonism perpetuates a monetary system which beggars you both.' Repeatedly he stressed the identity of interests that transcended differences in race, telling them that 'the colored tenant . . . is in the same boat with the white tenant, the colored laborer with the white laborer,' and that 'the accident of color can make no difference in the interests of farmers, croppers, and laborers.' He promised the Negroes that 'if you stand up for your rights and for your manhood, if you stand shoulder to shoulder with us in this fight' the People's party will 'wipe out the color line and put every man on his citizenship irrespective of color.'

To implement their promises the radicals went farther in the direction of racial integration than did the conservatives. 'We have no disposition to ostracize the colored people,' declared the president of the first Populist convention in Texas. 'I am in favor of giving the colored man full representation . . . He is a citizen just as much as we are, and the party that acts on that fact will gain the colored vote of the south.' The convention cheered these sentiments and elected two Negroes to the state executive committee of the party. Other Southern states followed the example of Texas. Negroes were not put off with nominal duties and peripheral appointments, but were taken into the inmost councils of the party. They served with Southern whites as members of state, district, and county executive committees, campaign committees, and delegations to national conventions. Black and white campaigners spoke from the same platform to audiences of both races, and both had their places on official party tickets. Populist sheriffs saw to it that Negroes appeared for jury duty; and Populist editors sought out achievements of Negroes to praise in their columns.

In the opinion of Henry Demarest Lloyd, the Southern Populists gave 'negroes of the South a political fellowship which they have never obtained, not even from their saviors, the Republicans.' Certain it is that the Negroes responded with more enthusiasm and hope than to any other political movement since their disillusionment with radical Republicanism. It is altogether probable that during the brief Populist upheaval of the 'nineties Negroes and native whites achieved a greater comity of mind and harmony of political purpose than ever before or since in the South.

The obvious danger in this account of the race policies of Southern conservatives and radicals is one of giving an exaggerated impression of interracial harmony. There were Negrophobes among the radicals as well as among the conservatives, and there were hypocrites and dissemblers in both camps. The politician who flatters to attract votes is a familiar figure in all parties, and the discrepancy between platforms and performance is often as wide as the gap between theory and practice, or the contrast between ethical ideals and everyday conduct.

My only purpose has been to indicate that things have not always been the same in the South. In a time when the Negroes formed a much larger proportion of the population than they did later, when slavery was a live memory in the minds of both races, and when the memory of the hardships and bitterness of Reconstruction was still fresh, the race policies accepted and pursued in the South were sometimes milder than they became later. The policies of proscription, segregation, and disfranchisement that are often described as the immutable 'folkways' of the South, impervious alike to legislative reform and armed intervention, are of a more recent origin. The effort to justify them as a consequence of Reconstruction and a necessity of the times is embarrassed by the fact that they did not originate in those times. And the belief that they are immutable and unchangeable is not supported by history.

III

Capitulation to Racism

Up to the year 1898 South Carolina had resisted the Jim Crow car movement which had swept the western states of the South completely by that time. In that year, however, after several attempts, the proponents of the Jim Crow law were on the eve of victory. The Charleston *News and Courier,* the oldest newspaper in the South and a consistent spokesman of conservatism, fired a final broadside against extremists in behalf of the conservative creed of race policy.

'As we have got on fairly well for a third of a century, including a long period of reconstruction, without such a measure,' wrote the editor, 'we can probably get on as well hereafter without it, and certainly so extreme a measure should not be adopted and enforced without added and urgent cause.' He then called attention to what he considered the absurd consequences to which such a law might lead once the principle of the thing were conceded. 'If there must be Jim Crow cars on the railroads, there should be Jim Crow cars on the street railways. Also on all passenger boats. . . . If there are to be Jim Crow cars, moreover, there should be Jim Crow waiting saloons at all stations, and Jim Crow eating houses. . . . There should be Jim Crow sections of the jury box, and a separate Jim Crow dock and witness stand in every court—and a Jim Crow Bible for colored witnesses to kiss. It would be advisable also to have a Jim Crow section in county auditors' and treasurers' offices for the accommodation of colored taxpayers. The two races are dreadfully mixed in these offices for weeks every year, especially about Christmas. . . . There should be a Jim Crow department for making returns and paying for the privileges and blessings of citizenship. Perhaps, the best plan would be, after all, to take the short cut to the general end . . . by establishing two or three Jim Crow counties at once, and turning them over to our colored citizens for their special and exclusive accommodation.'

In resorting to the tactics of *reductio ad absurdum* the editor doubtless believed that he had dealt the Jim Crow principle a telling blow with his heavy irony. But there is now apparent to us an irony in his argument of which the author was unconscious. For what he intended as a *reductio ad absurdum* and obviously regarded as an absurdity became in a very short time a reality, and not only that but a reality that was regarded as the only sensible solution to a vexing problem, a solution having the sanction of tradition and long usage. Apart from the Jim

Crow counties and Jim Crow witness stand, all the improbable applications of the principle suggested by the editor in derision had been put into practice—down to and including the Jim Crow Bible.

The South's adoption of extreme racism was due not so much to a conversion as it was to a relaxation of the opposition. All the elements of fear, jealousy, proscription, hatred, and fanaticism had long been present, as they are present in various degrees of intensity in any society. What enabled them to rise to dominance was not so much cleverness or ingenuity as it was a general weakening and discrediting of the numerous forces that had hitherto kept them in check. The restraining forces included not only Northern liberal opinion in the press, the courts, and the government, but also internal checks imposed by the prestige and influence of the Southern conservatives, as well as by the idealism and zeal of the Southern radicals. What happened toward the end of the century was an almost simultaneous—and sometimes not unrelated—decline in the effectiveness of restraint that had been exercised by all three forces: Northern liberalism, Southern conservatism, and Southern radicalism.

1

The acquiescence of Northern liberalism in the Compromise of 1877 defined the beginning, but not the ultimate extent, of the liberal retreat on the race issue. The Compromise merely left the freedman to the custody of the

conservative Redeemers upon their pledge that they
would protect him in his constitutional rights. But as
these pledges were forgotten or violated and the South
veered toward proscription and extremism, Northern
opinion shifted to the right, keeping pace with the South,
conceding point after point, so that at no time were the
sections very far apart on race policy. The failure of the
liberals to resist this trend was due in part to political
factors. Since reactionary politicians and their cause
were identified with the bloody-shirt issue and the demagogic exploitation of sectional animosities, the liberals
naturally felt themselves strongly drawn toward the
cause of sectional reconciliation. And since the Negro
was the symbol of sectional strife, the liberals joined in
deprecating further agitation of his cause and in defending the Southern view of race in its less extreme forms.
It was quite common in the 'eighties and 'nineties to
find in the *Nation, Harper's Weekly,* the *North American Review,* or the *Atlantic Monthly* Northern liberals
and former abolitionists mouthing the shibboleths of
white supremacy regarding the Negro's innate inferiority, shiftlessness, and hopeless unfitness for full participation in the white man's civilization. Such expressions
doubtless did much to add to the reconciliation of North
and South, but they did so at the expense of the Negro.
Just as the Negro gained his emancipation and new
rights through a falling out between white men, he now
stood to lose his rights through the reconciliation of
white men.

The cumulative weakening of resistance to racism was
expressed also in a succession of decisions by the United

States Supreme Court between 1873 and 1898 that require no review here. In the *Slaughter House Cases* of 1873 and in *United States* v. *Reese* and *United States* v. *Cruikshank* in 1876, the court drastically curtailed the privileges and immunities recognized as being under federal protection. It continued the trend in its decision on the *Civil Rights Cases* of 1883 by virtually nullifying the restrictive parts of the Civil Rights Act. By a species of what Justice Harlan in his dissent described as 'subtle and ingenious verbal criticism,' the court held that the Fourteenth Amendment gave Congress power to restrain states but not individuals from acts of racial discrimination and segregation. The court, like the liberals, was engaged in a bit of reconciliation—reconciliation between federal and state jurisdiction, as well as between North and South, reconciliation also achieved at the Negro's expense. Having ruled in a previous case (*Hall* v. *de Cuir*, 1877) that a state could not *prohibit* segregation on a common carrier, the Court in 1890 (*Louisville, New Orleans, and Texas Railroad* v. *Mississippi*) ruled that a state could constitutionally *require* segregation on carriers. In *Plessy* v. *Ferguson,* decided in 1896, the Court subscribed to the doctrine that 'legislation is powerless to eradicate racial instincts' and laid down the 'separate but equal' rule for the justification of segregation. Two years later, in 1898, in *Williams* v. *Mississippi* the Court completed the opening of the legal road to proscription, segregation, and disfranchisement by approving the Mississippi plan for depriving Negroes of the franchise.

For a short time after the Supreme Court decision of

1883 that held the restrictive parts of the Civil Rights
Act unconstitutional, Northern legislatures showed a
disposition to protect the rights of Negroes by state action. In the mid-'eighties thirteen states adopted civil
rights laws of this sort. In Indiana, however, a study by
Emma Lou Thornbrough finds that 'In practice the law
proved to be ineffectual in accomplishing its state purpose, and racial patterns [of segregation] remained unchanged by its passage.' The same historian goes further
to say that 'Throughout the North there was not only
acquiescence among the white population in the 'Southern Way' of solving the race problem but a tendency to
imitate it in practice.'

Then, in the year 1898, the United States plunged into
imperialistic adventures overseas under the leadership
of the Republican party. These adventures in the Pacific
and the Caribbean suddenly brought under the jurisdiction of the United States some eight million people
of the colored races, 'a varied assortment of inferior
races,' as the *Nation* described them, 'which, of course,
could not be allowed to vote.' As America shouldered the
White Man's Burden, she took up at the same time
many Southern attitudes on the subject of race. 'If the
stronger and cleverer race,' said the editor of the *Atlantic Monthly,* 'is free to impose its will upon "new-
caught, sullen peoples" on the other side of the globe,
why not in South Carolina and Mississippi?' The doctrines of Anglo-Saxon superiority by which Professor
John W. Burgess of Columbia University, Captain Alfred T. Mahan of the United States Navy, and Senator

Albert Beveridge of Indiana justified and rationalized American imperialism in the Philippines, Hawaii, and Cuba differed in no essentials from the race theories by which Senator Benjamin R. Tillman of South Carolina and Senator James K. Vardaman of Mississippi justified white supremacy in the South. The Boston Evening *Transcript* of 14 January 1899, admitted that Southern race policy was 'now the policy of the Administration of the very party which carried the country into and through a civil war to free the slave.' And *The New York Times* of 10 May 1900 reported editorially that 'Northern men . . . no longer denounce the suppression of the Negro vote [in the South] as it used to be denounced in the reconstruction days. The necessity of it under the supreme law of self-preservation is candidly recognized.'

In the South leaders of the white-supremacy movement thoroughly grasped and expounded the implication of the new imperialism for their domestic policies. 'No Republican leader,' declared Senator Tillman, 'not even Governor Roosevelt, will now dare to wave the bloody shirt and preach a crusade against the South's treatment of the negro. The North has a bloody shirt of its own. Many thousands of them have been made into shrouds for murdered Filipinos, done to death because they were fighting for liberty.' And the junior Senator from South Carolina, John J. McLaurin, thanked Senator George F. Hoar of Massachusetts 'for his complete announcement of the divine right of the Caucasian to govern the inferior races,' a position which 'most amply vindicated the South.' Hilary A. Herbert, an advocate of complete disfranchisement of the Negro in Alabama, re-joiced in May 1900 that 'we have now the sympathy of thoughtful men in the North to an extent that never be-fore existed.'

At the very time that imperialism was sweeping the country, the doctrine of racism reached a crest of ac-ceptability and popularity among respectable scholarly and intellectual circles. At home and abroad biologists, sociologists, anthropologists, and historians, as well as journalists and novelists, gave support to the doctrine that races were discrete entities and that the "Anglo-Saxon" or "Caucasian" was the superior of them all. It was not that Southern politicians needed any support from learned circles to sustain their own doctrines, but they found that such intellectual endorsement of their racist theories facilitated acceptance of their views and policies.

At the dawn of the new century the wave of Southern racism came in as a swell upon a mounting tide of na-tional sentiment and was very much a part of that senti-ment. Had the tide been running the other way, the Southern wave would have broken feebly instead of be-coming a wave of the future.

2

While northern and national restraints upon race ex-tremists were relaxing, internal Southern resistance was also crumbling. Such restraining influence as the con-servative tradition exercised upon race policy depended in large measure upon the power of Southern conservatives to retain the role of leadership that they had consolidated upon Redemption. They enjoyed enormous prestige for the overthrow of the carpetbaggers, a prestige that tided them over many of their difficulties. They contrived also to surround their regime with the protective mystique of the Lost Cause and to marshal for their support the powerful emotions of sectional patriotism that welled up out of the historic experiences of defeat, military occupation, and common suffering. Exploiting these advantages skillfully, the conservatives prolonged a remarkable tenure of office.

An accumulation of grievances and discontents gradually weakened their claim upon popular loyalty and undermined the authority of the conservative tradition. In the 'eighties a series of financial scandals in the Redeemer governments were exposed and the treasurers of seven states absconded or were charged with misappropriating funds. In some states, particularly Mississippi, the defalcations and pilfering outstripped the record of the carpetbaggers in this respect. Since the propaganda by which the Redeemers justified their overthrow of the carpetbaggers laid great stress upon corruption and dishonesty in office, and since one of the strongest claims of the Redeemers was impeccable honesty, the treasury scandals were especially embarrassing.

Another embarrassment that diminished the contrast between Redemption and Reconstruction was the conservative alliance with the Negro. In order to gain power to overthrow the carpetbaggers, the conservatives had enlisted the support of the aggressively anti-Negro whites in the struggle for redemption. That accomplished, the conservatives then attempted to moderate the passions of their Negrophobe allies and conciliate the freedmen with paternalistic offers of patronage and protection. The 'Straightout' or white-supremacy element often found the conservative tactics of pampering the Negro extremely difficult to stomach. When the General Assembly of North Carolina, under conservative control, elected several Negro magistrates for certain counties, nine white Democratic members signed a vigorous protest against the action as 'inconsistent with the principles and purposes of the party.' One of those principles, repeatedly expressed in the campaign for redemption, had been that Negroes were 'absolutely unfit for these public positions.' And, added the protest, 'If Democrats do what they have persistently abused and condemned Republicans for doing, how can they hope to escape just censure?' The 'Straightout' element of South Carolina, Mississippi, Louisiana, and other states similarly expressed their chagrin and even outrage over the soft race policy pursued by Hampton, Lamar, Nicholls, and their conservative colleagues.

Greater by far than either the financial scandals or the racial politics of the conservatives as a cause of their declining popularity were their economic policies and alliances. The Whiggish doctrines and ante-bellum associations of the Redeemers had never been among their more popular assets, and in the eyes of most Southerners they were liabilities. The Whigs had normally been the minority party aligned against the ante-bellum Democrats. Hamiltonian in outlook, they continued the Federalist tradition, constituted themselves champions of property rights and spokesmen of financial, commercial, and industrial interests. They broadened their appeal somewhat among the humble folk by demagogic devices and their opposition to the secession movement, but they continued to be known as the party of privilege. Before the war they had lent an agrarian ballast to the national party of the businessman. Their influence in the conservative Democratic party after the war, however, had been swung markedly on the side of corporate, industrial, and railroad interests. They struggled successfully to prevent the Southern Democrats from returning to their old alliance with the West and adopting Western notions about money, banks, railroads, and agrarian reforms. They were determined instead to keep the South in step with the conservative Northeastern wing of the party and with its views upon economic policy. Their reasoning was that the South's desperate need for capital and for industrialization justified any means to attract the confidence and interest of investors.

The storm of discontent aroused by the agrarian depression of the 'eighties and 'nineties caught the conservatives off guard and threw them on the defensive. A great restiveness seized upon the populace, a more profound upheaval of economic discontent than had ever moved the Southern people before, more profound in its political manifestations than that which shook them in the Great Depression of the 1930's. 'I call that particular change a revolution,' wrote the Alabama historian William Garrott Brown, who lived through it, 'and I would use a stronger term if there were one; for no other political movement—not that of 1776, nor that of 1860-1861—ever altered Southern life so profoundly.'

After trying rigid resistance, and appealing to party loyalty, Southern patriotism, and white solidarity without the desired effect, the conservatives bent to the storm to the extent of giving verbal assent to the program of reforms demanded by the aggressive Farmer's Alliance. But when they failed to carry through with their promises and live up to their pledges, the farmers accused them of betraying the cause, hastily organized a third party, and went into all-out revolt against the conservatives as well as the party they dominated. The Populists defied not only the conservative leaders but pretty much all they stood for, including the one-party system, the Eastern alliance, and white solidarity.

In their frantic efforts to stop the revolt and save themselves the conservatives lost their heads and sought to re-enact the triumph of earlier years by which they overthrew the carpetbaggers, redeemed the South, and won their laurels. They persuaded themselves that the crisis of the 'nineties was as desperate as that of the 'seventies had been. The South must be redeemed again, and the political ethics of redemption—which justified any means used to achieve the end—were pressed into service against the Populists as they had been against the carpetbaggers. The same means of fraud, intimidation, bribery, violence, and terror were used against the one that had been

used against the other. 'I told them to go to it, boys,
count them out,' admitted the conservative Governor
William C. Oates of Alabama. 'We had to do it. Unfortunately, I say it was a necessity. We could not help
ourselves.'

Alarmed by the success that the Populists were en-
joying with their appeal to the Negro voter, the conservatives themselves raised the cry of 'Negro domination' and white supremacy, and enlisted the Negrophobe
elements. The conservatives had allied themselves with
these elements before in the Redemption crisis, and then
later, after the crisis was over, they had been able to
tame the extremists into moderation. But they could no
longer claim in justification that they were using these
tactics against an alien element or even against a despised race. They were using them against their own
people, Southern white people. 'It is no excuse,' declared
a Virginia Populist paper in 1893, 'to say that these in-
iquities are practiced to "preserve white civilization." In
the first place it was white men who were robbed of
their votes, and white men who were defrauded out of
office.'

The conservatives compounded their offense and further weakened their moral authority with lower-class
white men by using the Negro vote against them. For
while they were raising a storm of race feeling against
the Populists with the charge that the insurgents were
using the Negro against the white man's party, the conservatives were taking advantage of their dominance in
the Black Belt to pile up huge majorities of Negro votes

for the cause of white supremacy. Some of these voters
were bought and some intimidated, but in the main they
were merely counted for the ticket, however they voted
or whether they voted or not. Time after time the Populists would discover that after they had carried the
white counties, fraudulent returns from the Black Belt
counties padded with ballots the Negro did or did not
cast were used to overwhelm them. When the conservatives in 1896 proved able to carry only one-fifth of the
parishes of Louisiana that had a white majority, the
New Orleans *Times-Democrat* cynically remarked that
white supremacy had again been 'saved by negro votes.'
The tactics by which the conservatives crushed the Populist revolt completely undermined their moral position
on race policy, for their methods had made a mockery
of the plea for moderation and fair play.

The Populist experiment in interracial harmony, precarious at best and handicapped from the start by suspicion and prejudice, was another casualty of the political crisis of the 'nineties. While the movement was at
the peak of zeal the two races had surprised each other
and astonished their opponents by the harmony they
achieved and the good will with which they co-operated.
When it became apparent that their opponents would
stop at nothing to divide them, however, and would
steal the Negro's votes anyway, the bi-racial partnership
of Populism began to dissolve in frustration and bitterness. Many of the Negroes became apathetic and ceased
political activity altogether. Some of the white Populists
understood that the Negro was merely one of the hapless

victims rather than the author of the party's downfall. But for the majority it came much easier to blame the Negro for their defeat, to make him the scapegoat, and to vent upon him the pent up accumulation of bitterness against the legitimate offenders who had escaped their wrath.

If the psychologists are correct in their hypothesis that aggression is always the result of frustration, then the South toward the end of the 'nineties was the perfect cultural seedbed for aggression against the minority race. Economic, political, and social frustrations had pyramided to a climax of social tensions. No real relief was in sight from the long cyclical depression of the 'nineties, an acute period of suffering that had only intensified the distress of the much longer agricultural depression. Hopes for reform and the political means employed in defiance of tradition and at great cost to emotional attachments to effect reform had likewise met with cruel disappointments and frustration. There had to be a scapegoat. And all along the line signals were going up to indicate that the Negro was an approved object of aggression. These 'permissions-to-hate' came from sources that had formerly denied such permission. They came from the federal courts in numerous opinions, from Northern liberals eager to conciliate the South, from Southern conservatives who had abandoned their race policy of moderation in their struggle against the Populists, from the Populists in their mood of disillusionment with their former Negro allies, and from a national temper suddenly expressed by imperialistic adventures and aggressions against colored peoples in distant lands.

The resistance of the Negro himself had long ceased to be an important deterrent to white aggression. But a new and popular spokesman of the race, its acknowledged leader by the late 'nineties, came forward with a submissive philosophy for the Negro that to some whites must have appeared an invitation to further aggression. It is quite certain that Booker T. Washington did not intend his so-called 'Atlanta Compromise' address of 1895 to constitute such an invitation. But in proposing the virtual retirement of the mass of Negroes from the political life of the South and in stressing the humble and menial role that the race was to play, he would seem unwittingly to have smoothed the path to proscription.

3

Having served as the national scapegoat in the reconciliation and reunion of North and South, the Negro was now pressed into service as a sectional scapegoat in the reconciliation of estranged white classes and the reunion of the Solid South. The bitter violence and blood-letting recrimination of the campaigns between white conservatives and white radicals in the 'nineties had opened wounds that could not be healed by ordinary political nostrums and free-silver slogans. The only formula powerful enough to accomplish that was the magical formula of white supremacy, applied without stint and without any of the old conservative reservations of paternalism, without deference to any lingering resistance of Northern liberalism, or any fear of further check from a defunct Southern Populism.

The first step in applying the formula was the total disfranchisement of the Negro. In part this was presented as a guarantee that in the future neither of the white factions would violate the white man's peace by rallying the Negro's support against the other. In part disfranchisement was also presented as a progressive reform, the sure means of purging Southern elections of the corruption that disgraced them. The disgrace and public shame of this corruption were more widely and keenly appreciated than the circuitous and paradoxical nature of the proposed reform. To one Virginian, however, it did seem that disfranchising the Negroes 'to prevent the Democratic election officials from stealing their votes' would be 'to punish the man who has been injured'—a topsy-turvy justice at best. In no mood for paradoxes, Southerners generally accepted Negro disfranchisement as a reform, without taking second thought.

The standard devices for accomplishing disfranchisement on a racial basis and evading the restrictions of the Constitution were invented by Mississippi, a pioneer of the movement and the only state that resorted to it before the Populist revolt took the form of political rebellion. Other states elaborated the original scheme and added devices of their own contriving, though there was a great deal of borrowing and interchange of ideas throughout the South. First of all, the plan set up certain barriers such as property or literacy qualifications for voting, and then cut certain loopholes in the barrier through which only white men could squeeze. The loopholes to appease (though not invariably accommodate) the underprivileged whites were the 'understanding clause,' the 'grandfather clause,' or the 'good character clause.' Some variation of the scheme was incorporated into the constitutions of South Carolina in 1895, Louisiana in 1898, North Carolina in 1900, Alabama in 1901, Virginia in 1902, Georgia in 1908, and Oklahoma in 1910. The restrictions imposed by these devices were enormously effective in decimating the Negro vote, but in addition all these states as well as the remaining members of the old Confederacy—Florida, Tennessee, Arkansas, and Texas—adopted the poll tax. With its cumulative features and procedures artfully devised to discourage payment, the poll tax was esteemed at first by some of its proponents as the most reliable means of curtailing the franchise—not only among the Negroes but among objectionable whites as well.

But if the Negroes did learn to read, or acquire sufficient property, and remember to pay the poll tax and to keep the receipt on file, they could even then be tripped by the final hurdle devised for them—the white primary. Another of the fateful paradoxes that seemed to dog the history of the progressive movement in the South, the primary system was undoubtedly an improvement over the old convention system and did much to democratize nominations and party control. But along with the progressively inspired primary system were adopted the oppositely inspired party rules, local regulations, and in some cases state laws excluding the minority race from participation and converting the primary into a white man's club. This perverse 'reform' usually followed hard upon, though sometimes preceded, the disfranchisement 'reform.' The state-wide Democratic primary was adopted in South Carolina in 1896, Arkansas in 1897, Georgia in 1898, Florida and Tennessee in 1901, Alabama and Mississippi in 1902, Kentucky and Texas in 1903, Louisiana in 1906, Oklahoma in 1907, Virginia in 1913, and North Carolina in 1915.

The effectiveness of disfranchisement is suggested by a comparison of the number of registered Negro voters in Louisiana in 1896, when there were 130,334 and in 1904, when there were 1,342. Between the two dates the literacy, property, and poll-tax qualifications were adopted. In 1896 Negro registrants were in a majority in twenty-six parishes—by 1900 in none.

In spite of the ultimate success of disfranchisement, the movement met with stout resistance and succeeded in some states by narrow margins or the use of fraud. In order to overcome the opposition and divert the suspicions of the poor and illiterate whites that they as well as the Negro were in danger of losing the franchise—a suspicion that often proved justified—the leaders of the movement resorted to an intensive propaganda of white supremacy, Negrophobia, and race chauvinism. Such a campaign preceded and accompanied disfranchisement in each state. In some of them it had been thirty years or more since the reign of the carpetbagger, but the legend of Reconstruction was revived, refurbished, and relived by the propagandists as if it were an immediate background of the current crisis. A new generation of Southerners was as forcibly impressed with the sectional trauma as if they had lived through it themselves. Symbols and paraphernalia of the Redemption drama were patched up and donned by twentieth-century wearers. Boys who had been born since General U. S. Grant was laid in his tomb paraded in the red shirts of their fathers, and popular Southern novelists glamorized the history of the Ku Klux Klan, the Knights of the White Camelia, and the heroes of the struggle for Home Rule.

In Georgia and elsewhere the propaganda was furthered by a sensational press that played up and headlined current stories of Negro crime, charges of rape and attempted rape, and alleged instances of arrogance, impertinence, surly manners, or lack of prompt and proper servility in conduct. Already cowed and intimidated, the race was falsely pictured as stirred up to a mutinous and insurrectionary pitch. The Atlanta *Journal,* edited by Hoke Smith while he was a candidate for governor on a disfranchisement platform, was one of the worst offenders in this regard. Throughout his campaign Smith's paper kept up a daily barrage of Negro atrocity stories.

It was inevitable that race relations should deteriorate rapidly under such pressure. The immediate consequences in two states were bloody mob wars upon the Negro. Shortly after the red-shirt, white-supremacy election of 1898 in North Carolina a mob of four hundred white men led by a former congressman invaded the colored district of Wilmington, set fire to buildings, killed and wounded many Negroes, and chased hundreds out of town. The sequel to Hoke Smith's white-supremacy victory in Georgia in 1906 was a four-day rule of anarchy in Atlanta, during which mobs roved the city freely looting, murdering, and lynching.

This ugly temper did not pass with the white-supremacy campaigns. Indeed the more defenseless, disfranchised, and intimidated the Negro became the more prone he was to the ruthless aggression of mobs. Three years after Tillman had completed his work of crushing Negro rights in South Carolina, colored people were victims of atrocities. While the state had accustomed itself peacefully to dozens of Negro postmasters before, the appointment of one in 1898 at Lake City touched off a mob that burned the postmaster up in his own house and shot down his family as they escaped. The same year mobs of 'white cap' riders ranged over the countryside of Greenwood County shooting and hanging an undetermined number of Negroes. Two years after the white-supremacy campaign had disfranchised the race in Louisiana, uncontrolled mobs took over the city of New Orleans and robbed and assaulted Negroes for three days. The number of lynchings per year was fortunately on the decline during the first decade of the century in the country as a whole and in the South. But the proportion of lynchings committed in the South was at the same time increasing, and so was the proportion of Negro victims of the lynchings committed.

A few of the old conservatives still spoke out against the savage turn that events had taken in race relations.

Wade Hampton announced during the disfranchisement campaign in South Carolina that he had 'no fear
of Negro domination,' that the Negroes had 'acted of late
with rare moderation,' and that race prejudice was being
exploited for the purposes of demagogues. But Hampton's influence had waned and he could do nothing to
stop the Tillmanites. Ex-Governor Oates of Alabama,
known as 'a conservative among conservatives' and once
the nemesis of Populism in his state, declared that he was
shocked at 'the change in public opinion in regard to
the status of the Negro' that had occurred by 1901. 'Why,
sir,' he declared to the disfranchising constitutional convention of Alabama, 'the sentiment is altogether different
now, when the Negro is doing no harm, why the people
want to kill him and wipe him from the face of the
earth.' But it was Governor Oates who had admitted to
the same body that in the heat of the Populist revolt he
had said, 'Go to it, boys. Count them out.' The admission weakened his moral position, as the conservative
tactic generally had undermined the authority of conservative influence on race relations.

Other representatives of the old conservative school,
such as Senator John T. Morgan of Alabama, gave aid
and comfort to the racists; or like Hoke Smith went over
to them lock, stock, and barrel, and became one of their
leaders. Younger men whose background, associations,
and ideas would have normally drawn them to the conservative, Hamptonian position on race in earlier days—
men such as John Sharp Williams of Mississippi, or
Furnifold M. Simmons of North Carolina, or later James

F. Byrnes of South Carolina—were swept up in the tide
of racist sentiment and gave voice to it.

White-supremacy leaders, however, measured their
success not by the number of conservative converts to
their cause, but by the response of the old Populists. For
if the racist strategy for the reconciliation of alienated
white men and the restoration of the Solid South were
to work, it would have to win the insurgents. Populists
were shrewdly watched for their reaction. In 1898, while
the Populists were still in control of the North Carolina
government, Josephus Daniels reported with elation seeing 'quite a number of white Populists and white Republicans' taking part in a red-shirt parade for white
supremacy. The following year when several Populist
members of the Legislature cast their votes for the disfranchisement amendment, 'the applause was long and
deafening, shouts and yells being added to the hand
clapping.' The reported yells were probably of the well-
known 'rebel' variety, for they hailed a closing of the
white man's ranks—white solidarity again.

Tom Watson, Populist candidate for President in
1904, was slower than some of his party to close ranks on
the race issue and capitulate to the extremists. He had
indignantly denounced the South Carolina disfranchisement campaign in 1895 with the statement that 'All this
reactionary legislation is wrong' and that 'Old fashioned
democracy taught that a man who fought the battles of
his country, and paid the taxes of his government, should
have a vote.' Bruised and embittered by another decade
of futile battles, he still believed that 'the bugaboo of

negro domination' was 'the most hypocritical that unscrupulous leadership could invent.' But by 1906 he had persuaded himself that only after the Negro was eliminated from politics could Populist principles gain a hearing. In other words, the white men would have to unite before they could divide. Watson optimistically believed that disfranchisement was the way to break up, rather than to unite, the Solid South. With that in view he offered to swing the Populist vote to any progressive Democratic candidate for governor who would run pledged to a platform of Populist reforms and Negro disfranchisement. Hoke Smith, a recent convert to progressivism from conservative ranks, took up the challenge and Watson delivered the Populist vote, with the results we have already reviewed. The picture of the Georgia Populist and the reformed Georgia conservative united on a platform of Negrophobia and progressivism was strikingly symbolical of the new era in the South. The campaign made Watson the boss of Georgia politics, but it wrote off Populism as a noble experiment, and launched its leader as one of the outstanding exploiters of endemic Negrophobia.

The omission of the South from the annals of the progressive movement has been one of the glaring oversights of American historians. Not only were all phases and aspects of the movement acted out below the Mason and Dixon line, but in some particulars the Southern progressives anticipated and exceeded the performance of their counterparts in the West and East. They chalked up some spectacular gains against the bosses and machines, the corporations and railroads, the insurance companies and trusts. They democratized politics with direct and preferential primaries, with corrupt-practices and anti-lobby acts, with initiative and referendum. They scored gains in humanitarian legislation for miners, factory workers, child labor, and the consumer.

The blind spot in the Southern progressive record—as, for that matter, in the national movement—was the Negro, for the whole movement in the South coincided paradoxically with the crest of the wave of racism. Still more important to the association of the two movements was the fact that their leaders were often identical. In fact, the typical progressive reformer rode to power in the South on a disfranchising or white-supremacy movement. Hoke Smith of Georgia is a case in point, but there were others. Charles B. Aycock and Josephus Daniels of North Carolina are two instances, and Carter Glass and Andrew J. Montague of Virginia are two more. And even those Southern progressives who gained power after the white-supremacy movement had triumphed—as was the case with Napoleon B. Broward of Florida and Braxton B. Comer of Alabama—were indebted to the movement, built upon it, and never repudiated it.

Racism was conceived of by some as the very foundation of Southern progressivism. Edgar Gardner Murphy, one of the most articulate and cultured of Southern progressives, thought of 'the conscious unity of race' as 'the broader ground of the new democracy,' and believed that despite all its limitations it was 'better as a basis of democratic reorganization than the distinctions of wealth, of trade, of property, of family, or class.' He praised 'the deep sociological value of what has been called "race prejudice" ' even though he earnestly deplored some of its results. Thomas P. Bailey, a Southern educator, conceived of progressivism as a direct corollary of racial proscription in the South. *'In fine,'* he wrote, *'disfranchisement of the negroes has been concomitant with the growth of political and social solidarity among the whites.* The more white men recognize sharply their kinship with their fellow whites, and the more democracy in every sense of the term spreads among them, the more the negro is compelled to "keep his place"—a place that is gradually narrowing in the North as well as in the South.'

The success of Woodrow Wilson's campaign for the presidential nomination and the management and direction of his race for President were in very considerable degree the work of an able school of Southern progressive politicians. Likewise the striking success of the progressive reforms of Wilson's first administration owed much of their vigor to the work of Southern cabinet members and congressional leaders. These Southern progressives also brought along to Washington with them the racial doctrines that left their stamp on the Wilsonian progressivism. One month before the election of Wilson, Josephus Daniels, then in charge of the publicity bureau of the Presidential campaign and soon to become a member of Wilson's cabinet, published an editorial in his North Carolina paper in which he said that the South would never feel secure until the North and West had adopted the whole Southern policy of political proscription and social segregation of the Negro.

4

Partisan politics was not the only index of the new trend in Southern race policy. A look at the contrast between Southern letters in the 1880's and in the 1900's also reveals something of the same development. The literary treatment that the Negro received in the fiction of Joel Chandler Harris and George Washington Cable was no doubt often patronizing, sentimentalized, and paternalistic, but there was never anything venomous or bitter about the Negro in their pages.* Rather the total picture that emerges is one that inspires a kind of respect, certainly sympathy, and more often an indulgent tenderness and affection. A stock figure to draw Southern tears was Uncle Remus with the little white boy in his lap, or the faithful black retainer of Marse Chan. It is instructive to compare the picture of the Negro painted by these authors who lived through Reconstruction themselves with the picture of the Negro during Reconstruction that emerges in the pages of Thomas Dixon, who was born the last year of the Civil War. Dixon was not of the same caliber as the earlier writers, but he accurately reflects the changed temper of the twentieth-century

---

* This claim cannot be advanced with the same assurance if extended to Harris's editorial writings, unsigned for the most part, in the Atlanta *Constitution*.

South. His trilogy: *The Leopard's Spots: A Romance of the White Man's Burden—1865-1900* (1902) ; *The Clansman: An Historical Romance of the Ku Klux Klan* (1905) ; and *The Traitor: A Story of the Fall of the Invisible Empire* (1907) was the perfect literary accompaniment of the white-supremacy and disfranchisement campaign, at the height of which they were published.

Scholarship of the period, particularly its sociology, anthropology, and history, likewise reflected the current deterioration in race relations and the new Southern attitudes. Charles Carroll, '*The Negro a Beast'; or, 'In the Image of God*' (1900) ; William P. Calhoun, *The Caucasian and the Negro in the United States* (1902) ; William B. Smith, *The Color Line: A Brief in Behalf of the Unborn* (1905) ; and Robert W. Shufeldt, *The Negro, A Menace to American Civilization* (1907) were a part of the then current national racist literature of the 'Yellow Peril' school and the flourishing cult of Nordicism. Southern historians during the first decade and a half of the century completed the rewriting of Reconstruction history. Their work did not yield completely to the contemporary atmosphere of the white-supremacy movement, but some of it did not entirely escape that influence.

Public-spirited professional people of a humanitarian bent who gathered at periodic conferences to discuss the race problem took a deeply pessimistic or despairing view of the Negro. They laid great stress on the alarming increase in Negro crime as the race flocked to the cities and packed into crowded, filthy slums. They were con-

vinced that the race was rapidly deteriorating in morals
and manners, in health and efficiency, and losing out in
the struggle for survival. They resolved that the Negro
was incapable of self-government, unworthy of the franchise, and impossible to educate beyond the rudiments.
They devoted much time and effort to the promotion of
Negro education, but the limitations of their aims are
indicated by Booker T. Washington when he said in
welcoming a conference of white Southern University
presidents to Tuskegee in 1912: 'We are trying to instil
into the Negro mind that if education does not make the
Negro humble, simple, and of service to the community,
then it will not be encouraged.'

Professor Paul B. Barringer of the University of Virginia told the Southern Education Association in 1900
that 'The negro race is essentially a race of peasant farmers and laborers . . . As a source of cheap labor for a
warm climate he is beyond competition; everywhere else
he is a foreordained failure, and as he knows this he de-
spises his own color.' 'Let us go back to the old rule of
the South', urged Barringer, 'and be done forever with
the frauds of an educational suffrage.' Southern sentiment in 1904 suggested to Carl Schurz 'a striking resem-
blance to the pro-slavery arguments . . . heard before
the Civil War, and they are brought forth . . . with the
same assertion of the negro's predestination for serfdom;
the same certainty that he will not work without "physical compulsion"; the same contemptuous rejection of
negro education as a thing that will only unfit him for
work.'

Wide agreement prevailed in the early years of the century that there was less sympathy, tolerance, and understanding between the races than there had been during the Reconstruction period, and some put the case even more strongly. Professor John Spencer Bassett of Trinity College wrote in 1903 that 'there is today more hatred of whites for blacks and blacks for whites than ever before.' John Temple Graves of Georgia said that 'The races are wider apart, more antagonistic than in 1865.' And the Negro novelist Charles W. Chestnutt said in 1903 that 'the rights of the Negroes are at a lower ebb than at any time during the thirty-five years of their freedom, and the race prejudice more intense and uncompromising.'

Such resistance to proscription and segregation as had lingered in the older states of the seaboard South crumbled rapidly. The Richmond *Times* in 1900 demanded that a rigid principle of segregation be 'applied in every relation of Southern life' on the ground that 'God Almighty drew the color line and it cannot be obliterated.' The conservative old Charleston *News and Courier,* quoted at the beginning of this chapter as heaping ridicule upon the Jim Crow movement and the absurdity of its consequences, was of another opinion by 1906. 'The "problem" is worse now than it was ten years ago,' wrote the editor. Far from being ridiculous, segregation did not now seem sufficient. Mass deportation was the remedy. 'Separation of the races is the only radical solution of the negro problem in this country . . . There is no room for them [the Negroes] here,' declared the paper.

5

Within this context of growing pessimism, mounting tension, and unleashed phobias the structure of segregation and discrimination was extended by the adoption of a great number of the Jim Crow type of laws. Up to 1900 the only law of this type adopted by the majority of Southern states was that applying to passengers aboard trains. And South Carolina did not adopt that until 1898,* North Carolina in 1899, and Virginia, the last, in 1900. Only three states had required or authorized the Jim Crow waiting room in railway stations before 1899, but in the next decade nearly all of the other Southern states fell in line. The adoption of laws applying to new subjects tended to take place in waves of popularity. Street cars had been common in Southern cities since the 'eighties, but only Georgia had a segregation law applying to them before the end of the century. Then in quick succession North Carolina and Virginia adopted such a law in 1901, Louisiana in 1902, Arkansas, South Carolina, and Tennessee in 1903, Mississippi and Maryland in 1904, Florida in 1905, and Oklahoma in 1907. These laws referred to separation within cars, but a Montgomery city ordinance of 1906 was the first to require a completely separate Jim Crow street car. During these years the older seaboard states of the South also extended the segregation laws to steamboats.

* For first-class coaches only, and not until 1900 was the law amended to apply to second class as well.

The mushroom growth of discriminatory and segregation laws during the first two decades of this century piled up a huge bulk of legislation. Much of the code was contributed by city ordinances or by local regulations and rules enforced without the formality of laws. Only a sampling is possible here. For up and down the avenues and byways of Southern life appeared with increasing profusion the little signs: 'Whites Only' or 'Colored.' Sometimes the law prescribed their dimensions in inches, and in one case the kind and color of paint. Many appeared without requirement by law — over entrances and exits, at theaters and boarding houses, toilets and water fountains, waiting rooms and ticket windows.

A large body of law grew up concerned with the segregation of employees and their working conditions. The South Carolina code of 1915, with subsequent elaborations, prohibited textile factories from permitting laborers of different races from working together in the same room, or using the same entrances, pay windows, exits, doorways, stairways, 'or windows [sic]' at the same time, or the same 'lavatories, toilets, drinking water buckets, pails, cups, dippers or glasses' at any time. Exceptions were made of firemen, floor scrubbers, and repair men, who were permitted association with the white proletarian elite on an emergency basis. In most instances segregation in employment was established without the aid of statute. And in many crafts and trades the written or unwritten policies of Jim Crow unionism made segregation superfluous by excluding Negroes from employment.

State institutions for the care of the dependent or in-
capacitated were naturally the subject of more legislation
than private institutions of the same sort, but ordinarily
the latter followed pretty closely the segregation practices
of the public institutions. Both types had usually made
it a practice all along. The fact that only Mississippi and
South Carolina specifically provided by law for general
segregation in hospitals does not indicate that non-segre-
gation was the rule in the hospitals of other states. The
two states named also required Negro nurses for Negro
patients, and Alabama prohibited white female nurses
from attending Negro male patients. Thirteen Southern
and border states required the separation of patients by
races in mental hospitals, and ten states specified segregation of inmates in penal institutions. Some of the latter
went into detail regarding the chaining, transportation,
feeding, and working of the prisoners on a segregated
basis. Segregation of the races in homes for the aged, the
indigent, the orphans, the blind, the deaf, and the dumb
was the subject of numerous state laws.

Much ingenuity and effort went into the separation
of the races in their amusements, diversions, recreations,
and sports. The Separate Park Law of Georgia, adopted
in 1905, appears to have been the first venture of a state
legislature into this field, though city ordinances and
local custom were quite active in pushing the Negro out
of the public parks. Circuses and tent shows, including
side shows, fell under a law adopted by Louisiana in
1914, which required separate entrances, exits, ticket
windows, and ticket sellers that would be kept at least

twenty-five feet apart. The city of Birmingham applied the principle to 'any room, hall, theatre, picture house, auditorium, yard, court, ball park, or other indoor or outdoor place' and specified that the races be 'distinctly separated . . . by well defined physical barriers.' North Carolina and Virginia interdicted all fraternal orders or societies that permitted members of both races to address each other as brother.

Residential segregation in cities, still rare in the older seaboard towns, developed along five different patterns in the second decade of the century. The type originating in Baltimore in 1910 designated all-white and all-Negro blocks in areas occupied by both races. This experiment was imitated in Atlanta and Greenville. Virginia sought to legalize segregation by a state law that authorized city councils to divide territories into segregated districts and to prohibit either race from living in the other's district, a method adopted by Roanoke and Portsmouth, Virginia. The third method, invented by Richmond, designated blocks throughout the city black or white according to the majority of the residents and forbade any person to live in any block 'where the majority of residents on such streets are occupied by those with whom said person is forbidden to intermarry.' This one was later copied by Ashland, Virginia, and Winston-Salem, North Carolina. A still more complicated law originated in Norfolk, which applied to both mixed and unmixed blocks and fixed the color status by ownership as well as occupancy. And finally New Orleans developed a law requiring a person of either race to secure consent

of the majority of persons living in an area before establishing a residence therein. After these devices were frus-
trated by a Supreme Court decision in 1917, attempts
continued to be made to circumvent the decision. Probably the most effective of these was the restrictive cove-
nant, a private contract limiting the sale of property in
an area to purchasers of the favored race.

The most prevalent and widespread segregation of
living areas was accomplished without need for legal
sanction. The black ghettos of the 'Darktown' slums in
every Southern city were the consequence mainly of the
Negro's economic status, his relegation to the lowest
rung of the ladder. Smaller towns sometimes excluded
Negro residents completely simply by letting it be known
in forceful ways that their presence would not be toler-
ated. In 1914 there were six such towns in Texas, five in
Oklahoma, and two in Alabama. On the other hand
there were by that time some thirty towns in the South,
besides a number of unincorporated settlements, in-
habited exclusively by Negroes. In August 1913, Clarence Poe, editor of the *Progressive Farmer,* secured the
unanimous endorsement of a convention of the North
Carolina Farmer's Union for a movement to segregate
the races in rural districts.

The extremes to which caste penalties and separation
were carried in parts of the South could hardly find a
counterpart short of the latitudes of India and South
Africa. In 1909 Mobile passed a curfew law applying exclusively to Negroes and requiring them to be off the
streets by 10 p.m. The Oklahoma legislature in 1915

authorized its Corporation Commission to require telephone companies 'to maintain separate booths for white
and colored patrons.' North Carolina and Florida required that textbooks used by the public-school children
of one race be kept separate from those used by the
other, and the Florida law specified separation even
while the books were in storage. South Carolina for a
time segregated a third caste by establishing separate
schools for mulatto as well as for white and Negro children. A New Orleans ordinance segregated white and
Negro prostitutes in separate districts. Ray Stannard
Baker found Jim Crow Bibles for Negro witnesses in
Atlanta courts and Jim Crow elevators for Negro passengers in Atlanta buildings.

6

A search of the statute books fails to disclose any state
law or city ordinance specifying separate Bibles and
separate elevators. Right here it is well to admit, and
even to emphasize, that *laws are not an adequate index
of the extent and prevalence of segregation and discriminatory practices in the South.* The practices often anticipated and sometimes exceeded the laws. It may be confidently assumed — and it could be verified by present
observation — that there is more Jim Crowism practiced
in the South than there are Jim Crow laws on the books.

To say that, however, is not to concede the position so
often taken by Southern as well as Northern writers that
the laws were of little consequence anyway. This view

consciously or unconsciously voices a laissez-faire bias and often leans for support upon the authority of William Graham Sumner. It was the contention of Sumner's classic *Folkways,* published in 1907, that 'legislation cannot make mores' and that 'stateways cannot change folkways.' Sumner described these 'folkways' as 'uniform, universal in the group, imperative, and invariable.' Perhaps it was not his intention, but Sumner's teachings lent credence to the existence of a primeval rock of human nature upon which the waves of legislation beat in vain. This concept as it was applied to Southern race practices and caste penalties was further buttressed by an American apostle of Herbert Spencer, the sociologist Franklin Henry Giddings. His emphasis upon 'consciousness of kind' in works appearing in 1896 and the decade following gave aid and comfort to the followers of Sumner. So did the racist interpretations of the psychologist William McDougall, whose *Introduction to Social Psychology* appeared in 1908.

Since the works mentioned represented the dominant American social theory of the early twentieth century, and since they appeared in the years when the wave of Southern and American racism was reaching its crest, it was natural that they should have influenced thinking upon the South's major social preoccupation. Their influence was to encourage the notion that there was something inevitable and rigidly inflexible about the existing patterns of segregation and race relations in the South; that these patterns had not been and could not be altered by conscious effort; and that it was, indeed, folly to attempt to meddle with them by means of legislation. These early twentieth-century theories have been characterized by a present-day psychologist, Kenneth B. Clark, as 'the modern attempt at acceptable restatement of the medieval doctrine of *innate ideas*.' Conceived of as biological or social imperatives, these modern 'innate ideas' were presented as 'folkways' or 'mores' which explained and, by inference, justified the existing structure of society, the privileges and policies of the dominant race, and the subordination of the minority race.

This body of social theory, though outmoded by later discovery and disproved by recent experience, continued to be pressed into use for various purposes down to quite recent times. Thus David L. Cohn of Mississippi wrote in the *Atlantic Monthly* of January 1944, 'It is William Graham Sumner's dictum that you cannot change the mores of a people by law, and since the social segregation of the races is the most deep-seated and pervasive of the Southern mores, it is evident that he who attempts to change it by law runs risks of incalculable gravity.' Among such risks he cited 'civil war' as one.

There was a curious contradiction or inconsistency implicit in the theory of this school in so far as it was applied to the history of race relations in the South. When William Graham Sumner wrote that 'The whites [in the South] have never been converted from the old mores' and that 'Vain attempts have been made to control the new order by legislation,' he was thinking of the legislative efforts of radical Reconstruction. Those were the laws he had in mind when he said that 'The only result is the proof that legislation cannot make mores.' It was the same experiment that the historian William H. Dunning, Giddings's colleague at Columbia, referred to in saying, 'The enfranchisement of the freedman was as reckless a species of statecraft, as that which marked "the blind hysterics of the Celt" in 1789–95.' And yet Southerners cited these authorities upon the utter futility of legislation in the alteration of relations between races to justify and support an elaborate program of legislation to change the relations between races in a different direction. The inference would seem to be that while sound scientific theory proved that folkways and mores could not be changed for some purposes, it proved at the same time that they could be changed for other purposes.

At any rate, the findings of the present investigation tend to bear out the testimony of Negroes from various parts of the South, as reported by the Swedish writer Gunnar Myrdal, to the effect that 'the Jim Crow statutes were effective means of tightening and freezing—in many cases instigating—segregation and discrimination.' The evidence has indicated that under conditions prevailing in the earlier part of the period reviewed the Negro could and did do many things in the South that in the latter part of the period, under different conditions, he was prevented from doing.

We have seen that in the 'seventies, 'eighties, and 'nineties the Negroes voted in large numbers. White leaders of opposing parties encouraged them to vote and earnestly solicited their votes. Qualified and acknowledged leaders of Southern white opinion were on record as saying that it was proper, inevitable, and desirable that they should vote. Yet after the disfranchisement measures were passed around 1900 the Negroes ceased to vote. And at that time qualified and acknowledged leaders of white opinion said that it was unthinkable that they should ever be permitted to vote. In the earlier decades Negroes still took an active, if modest, part in public life. They held offices, served on the jury, sat on the bench, and were represented in local councils, state legislatures, and the national Congress. Later on these things were simply not so, and the last of the Negroes disappeared from these forums.

It has also been seen that their presence on trains upon equal terms with white men was once regarded in some states as normal, acceptable, and unobjectionable. Whether railways qualify as folkways or stateways, black man and white man once rode them together and without a partition between them. Later on the stateways apparently changed the folkways—or at any rate the railways—for the partitions and Jim Crow cars became universal. And the new seating arrangement came to seem as normal, unchangeable, and inevitable as the old ways. And so it was with the soda fountains, bars, waiting rooms, street cars, and circuses. And so it probably was with the parks in Atlanta, and with cemeteries in Mississippi. There must even have been a time in Oklahoma when a colored man could walk into any old telephone booth he took a notion to and pick up the receiver.

What was once said in extenuation of the harshness of

the black codes of slavery times—that they were more honored in the breach than in the observance—cannot be said of the Jim Crow codes. Any Southerner of middle age, of course, could think of exceptions: the old 'auntie' who came to talk with one's grandmother on Saturday afternoons when the weather was nice; the privileged 'uncle' who preferred and was permitted to attend the white church; the defiant 'mammy' on the white day coach; and the old retainer who lorded it over the family larder and put the grocer's white delivery boy in his place. But we recognize them all as belated survivors of the old times — relics now gone with the second wind of history.

Barring those disappearing exceptions, the Jim Crow laws applied to *all* Negroes—not merely to the rowdy, or drunken, or surly, or ignorant ones. The new laws did not countenance the old conservative tendency to distinguish between classes of the race, to encourage the 'better' element, and to draw it into a white alliance. Those laws backed up the Alabamian who told the disfranchising convention of his state that no Negro in the world was the equal of 'the least, poorest, lowest-down white man I ever knew'; but not ex-Governor Oates, who replied: 'I would not trust him as quickly as I would a negro of intelligence and good character.' The Jim Crow laws put the authority of the state or city in the voice of the street-car conductor, the railway brakeman, the bus driver, the theater usher, and also into the voice of the hoodlum of the public parks and playgrounds. They gave free rein and the majesty of the law to mass aggressions that might otherwise have been curbed, blunted, or deflected.

The Jim Crow laws, unlike feudal laws, did not assign the subordinate group a fixed status in society. They were constantly pushing the Negro farther down. In seeking to distinguish between the Southern white attitudes toward the Negro during Reconstruction and the era following and the attitudes later developed, Edgar Gardner Murphy in 1911 called the one 'defensive' and 'conservative' and the other 'increasingly aggressive' and 'destructive.' 'The new mood,' he wrote, 'makes few professions of conservatism. It does not claim to be necessary to the state's existence . . . These new antipathies are not defensive, but assertive and combative . . . frankly and ruthlessly destructive.' The movement had proceeded in mounting stages of aggression. 'Its spirit is that of an all-absorbing autocracy of race, an animus of aggrandizement which makes, in the imagination of the white man, an absolute identification of the stronger race with the very being of the state.'

We have come a long way since that time and since that mood prevailed in the South. But most of the distance we have traveled has been covered in very recent years. The most common observation upon recent developments in race relations by intelligent white people of the South is almost invariably prefaced by the phrase: 'Ten (or twenty) years ago I would never have believed that . . .' And, indeed, there was then little reason to believe, or to expect, that things would change in the

South at any more than a glacial pace. For as recently as that the doctrine according to Sumner prevailed almost unchallenged in the mind of the laity — as well as in the minds of a good part of the 'experts' on social problems. And that doctrine had it that however crying the need for change, those immovable 'folkways' and irresistible 'mores' made the whole idea impracticable, or slowed down change to the pace of evolution.

When a scientific theory ceases to account for the observed facts of common experience, however, it would seem to be time to discard the theory. In lieu of another to offer in its place, we can at least try to understand what has happened.

IV
The Man on the Cliff

In the second year of the First World War, Maurice S. Evans, an Englishman who made his home in South Africa, wrote a book on race relations in the South that, according to the subtitle, was written 'From a South African Point of View.' He found conditions in the South 'strikingly similar' to those he had left behind at home. 'The separation of the races in all social matters,' he wrote, 'is as distinct in South Africa as in the Southern States. There are separate railway cars . . . and no black man enters hotel, theatre, public library or art gallery.' There were also in his homeland the same separate schools, the same disfranchisement, and the same political and economic subordination of the black man. 'How often,' he exclaimed, 'the very conditions I had left were reproduced before my eyes, the thousands of miles melted away, and Africa was before me.' Evans thought that 'in essence the problem is the same for both

of us'—South Africa and the Southern states of America
—and that the two great regions should and probably
would pursue much the same course toward the solution
of their common problems in the future. He particularly
urged upon the South 'a separation of the races such as is
still possible to us in South Africa,' where 'we still have
the black States.' He believed that this solution would
be worth 'heavy sacrifices to ensure it.'

At the time of the First World War there was much to
lend plausibility to Evans's prediction that the South
and South Africa would follow parallel courses in the
future. And there was at that time little evidence to indicate that their paths would eventually come to a point
of sharp divergence. Thoughtful Southerners such as
Alfred H. Stone, a planter from the Yazoo delta of Mississippi, were conscious of the parallel between the policies pursued by the dominant whites of the two regions.
'There are more Negroes in Mississippi,' wrote Stone,
than in Cape Colony, or Natal, even with the great territory of Zululand annexed to the latter; more than in
the Transvaal, and not far from as many as in both the
Boer colonies combined.' He remarked that the movement for disfranchisement had been 'simultaneously
agitated in both Cape Colony and Mississippi,' and that
action on the subject in the colony had followed hard
upon that in his state, with an interval of only two years
between them.

1

There was as yet no sign of a revival of Northern resistance to Southern race policy. If anything, thought Thomas P. Bailey, Northern opposition was still on the decline. In his *Race Orthodoxy in the South*, published in 1914, Bailey asked: 'Is not the South being *encouraged* to treat the negroes *as aliens* by the growing discrimination against the negro in the North, a discrimination that is social as well as economic? Does not the South perceive that all the fire has gone out of the Northern philanthropic fight for the rights of man? *The North has surrendered!*' According to Bailey it was 'the underlying feeling of many a Southern leader' that ' "They are going to let us alone; we'll fix things to suit ourselves." ' The trend in the North, he believed, was toward the adoption of the Southern Way as the American Way. 'Even now,' he observed, 'the solid Far West is joining hands with the South in racial matters; and the end is not yet in the growing solidarity of the white people in this country.'

The concentration upon the South in these pages should not lead to the inference that the attitudes and policies described here were peculiar to the South. Indeed, if the evidence had been collected in authoritative studies, it would be a simple matter to point out the many parallel lines of prejudice and discrimination against the Negro in the North, prejudice that often worked as great a hardship upon the race as it did in the

South. The trend toward racism in the North was amply illustrated in the years immediately following the First World War.

The war aroused in the Negroes a new hope for restoration of their rights and a new militancy in demanding first-class citizenship. More than 360,000 of them entered military service and a large part of those saw overseas duty in uniform. More joined the exodus of migration to the North in quest of high wages in the war industries. Temporary prosperity gave them new hopes and desires that needed fulfillment, and official propaganda picturing American participation in the war as a crusade for democracy raised the natural demand for a little more democracy at home.

The war-bred hopes of the Negro for first-class citizenship were quickly smashed in a reaction of violence that was probably unprecedented. Some twenty-five race riots were touched off in American cities during the last six months of 1919, months that John Hope Franklin called 'the greatest period of interracial strife the nation had ever witnessed.' Mobs took over cities for days at a time, flogging, burning, shooting, and torturing at will. When the Negroes showed a new disposition to fight and defend themselves, violence increased. Some of these atrocities occurred in the South—at Longview, Texas, for example, or at Tulsa, Oklahoma, at Elaine, Arkansas, or Knoxville, Tennessee. But they were limited to no one section of the country. Many of them occurred in the North and the worst of all in Chicago. During the first year following the war more than seventy Negroes were lynched, several of them veterans still in uniform.

In the postwar era there were new indications that the Southern Way was spreading as the American Way in race relations. The great migration of Negroes into the residential slum areas and the industrial plants of the big Northern cities increased tension between races. Northern labor was jealous of its status and resentful of the competition of Negroes, who were excluded from unions. Negroes were pushed out of the more desirable jobs in industries that they had succeeded in invading during the manpower shortage of the war years. They were squeezed out of federal employment more and more. Negro postmen began to disappear from their old routes, as Negro policemen did from their old beats. They began to lose their grip upon crafts such as that of the barbers, which had once been a virtual monopoly in the South.

Racism in regimented form was spread over the whole country in the 'twenties by the new Ku Klux Klan. Organized in Georgia in 1915, the new Klan did not reach its peak of membership, reported to have been five million, until the mid-twenties. Directed against other racial and religious minorities, as well as against the Negro, the Klan attained a larger following outside the South than within. Its influence within the South, however, toward the inflaming of prejudice, the encouragement of race violence, and the strengthening of the segregation code was powerful. At least two state governments, those of Texas and Oklahoma, were for a time almost completely under the domination of the Klan. Though the formal organization declined rapidly before the end of the 'twenties, sporadic outbreaks of its activities continued in the lower South into recent times.

There was no apparent tendency toward abatement or relaxation of the Jim Crow code of discrimination and segregation in the 1920's, and none in the 'thirties until well along in the depression years. In fact the Jim Crow laws were elaborated and further expanded in those years. Much social and economic history is reflected in the new laws. When women began to bob their hair and become patrons of the barber shops, Atlanta passed an ordinance in 1926 forbidding Negro barbers to serve women or children under fourteen years of age. Jim Crow kept step with the march of progress in transportation and industry, as well as with the changes in fashion. Mississippi brought her transportation laws abreast of the times in 1922 by passing a state-wide Jim Crow law applying to taxicabs. City ordinances requiring Jim Crow taxis were adopted by Jacksonville in 1929, by Birmingham in 1930, and by Atlanta in 1940. The Atlanta law required signs 'in an oil paint of contrasting color' painted on the vehicle to indicate which race it served, and further specified that 'There shall be white drivers for carrying white passengers and colored drivers for carrying colored passengers.' The advent of the cross-country buses as serious competitors of the railways was marked by the extension of the Jim Crow train law to the buses in all particulars, including seating arrangement, waiting rooms, toilets, and

other accommodations. The arrival of the age of air
transportation appears to have put a strain upon the
ingenuity of the Jim Crow lawmakers. Even to the or-
thodox there was doubtless something slightly incon-
gruous about requiring a Jim Crow compartment on a
transcontinental plane, or one that did not touch the
ground between New York and Miami. No Jim Crow
law has been found that applies to passengers while they
are in the air. So long as they were upon the ground,
however, they were still subject to Jim Crow jurisdiction. The Virginia legislature empowered the State Corporation Commission in 1944 to require separate waiting rooms and other facilities in airports. Air companies
generally complied with custom without the compulsion
of law—at least so far as activities on the ground were
concerned.

In the field of recreation, sports, and amusements the
laws continued to be tightened. An Atlanta ordinance
of June 1940 made the single exception of its park segregation 'so much of Grant park as is occupied by the zoo.'
Only in the presence of the lower anthropoids could
law-abiding Atlantans of different races consort together.
The same city in 1932 prohibited amateur baseball clubs
of different races from playing within two blocks of each
other. In 1933 Texas prohibited 'Caucasians' and 'Afri-
cans' from boxing and wrestling together. Federal law
stepped in to hinder the circulation of films showing
interracial boxing. An Arkansas law of 1937 required
segregation at all race tracks and gaming establishments
'in seating, betting, and all other accommodations.' In

1935 Oklahoma extended the white man's law to separate the races while fishing or boating. A Birmingham
ordinance got down to particulars in 1930 by making it
'unlawful for a Negro and a white person to play together or in company with each other' at dominoes or
checkers.

By 1944 the Swedish writer Gunnar Myrdal observed
that 'Segregation is now becoming so complete that the
white Southerner practically never sees a Negro except
as his servant and in other standardized and formalized
caste situations.'

2

Tension between the races eased somewhat during the
'thirties while both white and colored people grappled
with the problems of the Great Depression. For the first
time in history the great majority of both races in the
South joined the same political party. Under a liberal
administration that party appeared to be sincerely striving to improve the lot of the black man as well as that of
the white man. In spite of unyielding segregation, a few
new opportunities opened to the Negro in cultural life,
housing, health improvement, and education through
federal agencies of the New Deal. Interracial violence,
particularly lynching, declined markedly. Southern
white people and even the liberals among them were
beginning to congratulate themselves upon the dawn
of what seemed to be a new and hopeful era of interracial relations.

Then, quite abruptly and unaccountably—or so it

seemed to many Southern white people—an avalanche of
denunciation, criticism, and opprobrium descended
upon the South from above the Mason and Dixon line.
Militant and organized demands from both Negro and
white sources of pressure were raised for immediate
abolition of segregation. There was an aggressiveness
about the new agitation that frightened the South. Coming on the heels of what some Southerners had considered a period of relative progress in racial relations, the
demands seemed the more unreasonable and unfair.
They coincided with the war crisis that had already
frayed people's nerves. It was sometimes hard to tell
whether the international or the interracial conflict excited the bitterest feeling. Howard W. Odum in his
Race and Rumors of Race has vividly described the atmosphere of suspicion and fear that brooded over the
South in the early 'forties. The flying rumors of plot and
counterplot, of bands armed with icepick and switch-
blade knife, of Eleanor Clubs, conspiratorial societies,
and subversive Northern agitators often recall the fe-
vered frame of mind that possessed the South in the win-
ter following the Harpers Ferry raid. To the experienced sociologist Odum, it seemed that 'the South and
the Negro in the early 1940's, faced their greatest crisis
since the days of the reconstruction and that many of
the same symbols of conflict and tragedy that were manifest in the 1840's were evident again a hundred years
later.'

Responsible spokesmen of the South, gravely alarmed,
felt it necessary to issue stern warnings. 'A small group

of Negro agitators and another small group of white rabble-rousers,' wrote Virginius Dabney in January 1943, 'are pushing this country closer and closer to an interracial explosion which may make the race riots of the First World War and its aftermath seem mild by comparison. Unless saner counsels prevail, we may have the worst internal clashes since Reconstruction, with hundreds, if not thousands, killed and amicable race relations set back for decades.' Other writers invoked the Sumnerian imperative of the incorrigible folkways to stem the tide of agitation. 'A fact as sure as science,' declared John Temple Graves, 'is that the white majorities of the South are unwavering and total in their determination not to have race segregation abolished.' According to David L. Cohn, 'Southern whites, therefore, will not at any foreseeable time relax the taboos and conventions which keep the races separate, from the cradle to the grave.' And in the words of Mark Ethridge, 'There is no power in the world—not even in all the mechanized armies of the earth, Allied and Axis—which could now force Southern white people to the abandonment of the principle of social segregation.'

With the advantage of hindsight that these gentlemen did not enjoy, we now know that things did not turn out in quite the way these pessimistic utterances predicted. The interracial explosion that would have made the riots following the First World War mild by comparison fortunately did not materialize. And furthermore, despite the Sumnerian imperative, the incorrigible taboos and mores have in the meantime relaxed perceptibly at several points between the cradle and the grave. In fact, the point in the mid-'forties that was so confidently proclaimed to be the *ne plus ultra* of Southern tolerance actually marked the beginning of the period of most rapid advance against the walls of segregation that has yet been made—an advance that does not yet appear to have been halted.

At some point along their parallel ways it is now clear that the paths of the South and of South Africa diverged. At the time of the First World War it had seemed that both regions were going roughly the same way. But by the time the Second World War was over it was very plain that they were no longer traveling together. Indeed, as the tragic destination of South Africa became more and more apparent, and as more hopeful events transpired on the other side of the Atlantic, it began to seem as if the two great regions might be traveling in opposite directions.

In its plight the South might have cast a glance back over its shoulder to South Africa, with which it once identified itself and seemed to see eye to eye. Alan Paton, a son of South Africa, has described what he calls the 'tragic dilemma' of the white man in Paton's native land. 'A man is caught on the face of a cliff,' he writes. 'As he sees it, he cannot go up and he cannot go down; if he stays where he is, he will die. All those who stand watching have pity for him. But the analogy, alas, is obviously incomplete, for the world's spectators of our drama are seldom pitiful; they are more often reproachful. From their point of vantage they can see which way we ought to go, but they see us taking some other way which will lead us to destruction. And . . . the world looks at us in astonishment, wondering what madness has possessed us.'

The South no longer identified herself with South Africa and no longer had reason to fear the madness of self destruction. The South somewhere along the way took a different path. It had joined the spectators who were watching the tragic dilemma of the man on the cliff. But the South would watch with more pity and less reproachfulness than some of the spectators. For the South still had its own dilemmas, and the spectators had expanded to a world audience. The South's dilemmas might no longer be tragic, but they were none the less real, and the spectators were still reproachful.

Historians will long dispute the turning point of the South and the reasons for the momentous change of course. The first who attempt to plot the course and explain the change will make mistakes in emphasis and interpretation that will probably seem ludicrous to those who will later have the advantage of hindsight and perspective. But someone has to make a beginning.

3

For almost a century now historians have disputed the decisive factors that led to the first era of emancipation and Reconstruction. To some it has seemed that ideas and their propagation and dissemination have been the important influences. Such historians have naturally stressed the roles of the agitator, the propagandist, and the pressure group. They have dwelt at length upon the abolitionist crusade and the various anti-slavery leaders —their societies, tactics, and the influence these have had upon the course of events. Other writers have deprecated the importance of such influences and have instead laid greater stress upon impersonal, amoral, and non-volitional forces of history. Such people have emphasized the part played by conflicting commercial, industrial, and financial interests of large groups, the blind surges of mass emotions, the exigencies of party politics, and the harsh expedients of modern warfare. No really capable historian has entirely neglected any of these forces, and the better of them have attempted syntheses of all. But they have so far not arrived at a consensus that has met with anything approaching general endorsement.

All the various forces, moral and amoral, whose importance the historians have disputed in explaining the first era of emancipation and Reconstruction have their counterparts in the historical background of the movement we are presently attempting to understand. For the modern development also has a background of ideas, propaganda, agitation, and pressure groups as well as a background of conflicting economic interests, power politics, and war. In both the nineteenth-century and the twentieth-century movements, emotional factors of race prejudice and sectional pride, as well as the compulsions of frustration and aggression, have played their parts. It will long be a matter of debate as to the relative importance played by the agitators, foreign and domestic propaganda, the courts, the White House, party politics, two or three wars, postwar prosperity, the seemingly interminable Cold War, or the dubious influence of nationalism and oppressive conformity working in a new direction. It would be foolhardy to attempt, with no more than the foreshortened and distorting perspective we now have, to arrive at anything more than a very tentative assessment of the bewilderingly complex forces involved and the relative importance of the part each has played.

The evaluation of ideas and their agitation is most difficult because of the impossibility of measuring the results. It is clear at least that the Negro himself played a larger role in the new movement for emancipation than he had in the abolitionist crusade that led to the original emancipation. There were strange movements such as those led by Marcus Garvey and 'Father Divine,' but the majority of the more intelligent Negro agitators identified themselves with such organizations as the National Association for the Advancement of Colored People. An interracial organization founded in 1909, the N.A.A.C.P. performed effective work in agitating against discrimination and lynching, but gained no mass support or powerful influence for the first decade or more. Between the First and Second World Wars, however, the number of local chapters increased from about fifty to more than ten times that number. Claiming a large membership, the association became a power to be reckoned with in national politics. In the meantime the National Urban League had been established in forty-eight cities. These organizations attracted powerful support from the white world, without which they could never have achieved what they did.

Of great importance in arousing the sympathy and stimulating the support of white intellectuals and philanthropists was the Negro literary and artistic awakening of the 'twenties and early 'thirties sometimes called the 'Harlem Renaissance.' A sudden outpouring of formidable proportions, some of it good and some bad, the Negro fiction, poetry, and song was highly race-conscious and inspired by the spirit of protest. New poets and novelists gained national attention by giving voice to the ancient wrongs, the brooding sorrows, and the mounting indignation of their race. White admirers patronized and encouraged their efforts with publicity and funds. Negro art for a time enjoyed an enormous vogue, and the Negro himself acquired a prestige as a *cause célèbre* among intellectuals and the philanthropically inclined, a prestige second only to that of the proletariat in the 'thirties. When the proletariat became less fashionable, the Negro remained the residuary repository of thwarted humanitarianism.

Religious sentiment is not to be neglected in the briefest sketch of the agitation for Negro rights. The 'social gospel' movement began to permeate the great Southern Protestant sects in the early years of the century. As the breach between the estranged Northern and Southern branches of Methodism and the other churches healed more firmly in the 'thirties, the extension of the social gospel to include the Negro and his wrongs made itself felt more strongly in the Southern connections. The more solidly organized Roman Catholics simultaneously moved in the same direction. By the 1940's some relatively advanced pronouncements were coming from religious sources in the South.

The American faith in equality of opportunity and equality of rights has never really known any sectional boundaries. It has been professed as devoutly in the South as elsewhere, even by those who know their racial views are inconsistent with the national faith and acknowledge that the status accorded the Negro represents a lag in public morals. It has been the avowed mission (timidly pursued) of Southern liberals to sting the conscience of the South into an intensified awareness of the inconsistency between creed and custom. By the fourth decade of the twentieth century there had grown up in the South a considerable body of indigenous urban liberal strength that was gaining influence. Avowed liberals such as Ralph McGill for the first time began to direct the editorial policies of some of the oldest and strongest Southern newspapers. Southern liberals also began to appear in the highest political offices, on the floor of the Senate, on the Supreme Court bench, and in advisory offices close to the White House.

One of the earliest vehicles of liberal influence in the South was the Commission on Interracial Cooperation, organized in 1919, 'to quench, if possible, the fires of racial antagonism which were flaming at that time.' Moderate in tone, the commission emphasized an educational program and directed its attack against lynching and discrimination, but not segregation. The tradition established by the commission has been ably promoted by its successor, the Southern Regional Council, founded in 1944. More militant and radical than either of these was the Southern Conference for Human Welfare, which was launched in 1938 with an aggressive program in behalf of all underprivileged groups. Chief among these groups was, naturally, the Negro, and the demands made in his behalf were not limited by the same deference to prevailing opinion that earlier Southern agitators had shown.

The twentieth-century crusade for Negro rights began about as long before the practical politicians took it up as did the nineteenth-century abolitionist crusade. But unlike the abolitionists, whose fervor reached its climax more than two decades before their program achieved practical consummation, the modern crusaders have sustained a mounting crescendo of enthusiasm and pressure. The flood of anti-slavery petitions and bills that reached its crest and all but stopped the wheels of Congress in the mid-1830's had subsided to a trickle in the 1850's. On the other hand, in the recent period, while only ten bills favorable to civil rights were introduced in the Seventy-fifth Congress (1937-38), the number of such bills increased in each succeeding Congress until in the Eighty-first Congress (1949-50) seventy-two were introduced.

It is evident from many other indications that before this time the practical politicians and strategists of the two great political parties were interested in a movement that agitators and propagandists had started. To understand why this happened, just as to understand why abolitionism became involved in practical politics, we must turn from the realm of ideas, moral principles, and their agitators to the sphere of the more amoral and impersonal forces.

Several of these forces have enormously swelled the great migration of Negroes from the South in recent years. In the decade of the 'forties alone the number of Negroes living outside the South jumped from 2,360,000 to 4,600,000, an increase of nearly 100 per cent. At the present time more than one-half of the Negroes in the country live outside the South, as compared with about one-tenth sixty-five years ago. Most of this increase has gone to the industrial states, where the Negro population increased from five to ten times as fast as the white between 1940 and 1950. Within the South in that same decade, on the other hand, the white-population increase proved to be thirty-three times as great as the gain in the number of Negroes. What the South has long claimed as its peculiar problem was no longer a regional monopoly, but a national problem.

These population changes have had many implications for the changes in the Negro's status and the movement for his rights. The Northern Negro population is largely urban and the Southern Negroes are increasingly so. The importance of civil rights and the laws that define and protect them increases for the Negro in proportion to his urbanization. His power for making effective political demand for his rights has also increased as he has moved northward and cityward.

The shift in Negro population has had far-reaching political implications, for the Negroes outside the South were located mainly in closely contested urban centers and industrial states. But instead of dividing their votes between the two great parties and becoming, as their leaders hoped, a 'balance of power' that would compel both parties to bid for their support, the Negroes have flocked fairly solidly to the Democratic standard and cast off their historic allegiance to the Republican party. The result has been something like a reversal of the traditional position of the two major parties toward the Negro, as a survey of the elections since 1948 would indicate. The party of white supremacy had become on the national plane the outspoken champion of Negro rights, while the party of emancipation had been left free to seek alliance in the South with the disaffected white-supremacy leaders. At the same time the strategic location of the Negro minority in the North had made it sometimes more important to the success of the Democratic party in national elections than the disaffected whites in the Southern wing of the Democracy. The effect of this reversal had been unmistakably registered in the national Democratic platforms since 1948 as well as in the domestic policies and pronouncements of Presidents Franklin D. Roosevelt and Harry S. Truman.

In spite of the prosperity boom of the war and postwar years which has scattered wealth so profusely, the great majority of lower-class Negroes still live close to the subsistence level of existence. An urban middle class of the race, however, has benefited by a share of the prosperity and has entered the competitive struggle to achieve and maintain middle-class living standards and climb up in the world. Rather sharply differentiated from the lower class of the race, the Negro middle class has made a strong bid for the respect and deference of the white world. This bid was registered in dress and speech, in consumer habits, as well as in conduct. Such courtesy and deference as they have won may have been in considerable measure inspired by competition for the increased purchasing power of the Negro, but that has not been the only source. These people have begun to produce talent in the arts, in academic life, and in politics that has done much to reinforce their claim to a rise in status. Another effect of the prosperity boom has been that the South has begun to pull out of its seventy-five-year stalemate of an underprivileged and colonial economy. In the process the South has begun to find that it is easier to share prosperity than poverty with the minority race.

War and international tension, as well as the business cycle, have made their impact felt upon the pattern of racial relations in the South. The foremost of the Axis powers against which the United States fought in the Second World War was the most forceful exponent of racism the modern world has known. The Nazi crime against the minority race, more than anything else, was the offense against the Western moral code that branded the Reich as an outlaw power. Adolf Hitler's doctrine of the 'master race' had as its chief victim the Jew, but the association of that doctrine with the creed of white supremacy was inevitably made in the American mind. The association is not likely to be broken very easily. American war propaganda stressed above all else the abhorrence of the West for Hitler's brand of racism and its utter incompatibility with the democratic faith for which we fought. The relevance of this deep stirring of the American conscience for the position of the Negro was not lost upon him and his champions. Awareness of the inconsistency between practice at home and propaganda abroad placed a powerful lever in their hands.

Almost as soon as the crusade against Hitler and the Axis powers was concluded, we found ourselves locked in the grip of a Cold War with a former ally. Communist propaganda had long used stories of racial discrimination and injustice to discredit American capitalism and democracy in the eyes of the world. This issue gained tremendously in poignancy when the two powers faced each other in an ideological struggle for world leadership. It came near the focus of antagonism when the center of rivalry between Russia and America shifted to Asia and the two systems began to contend desperately for the friendship of the great colored races of the Orient. In this struggle the issue of segregation, far from being confined to regional boundaries, became international in scope. The daily press of Tokyo, Delhi, Peiping and Saigon was diligently searched in our State

Department for reactions to the latest outburst of inter-racial violence in Florida or Detroit, or the latest Supreme Court decision on segregation.

In a brief filed in December 1952 with the Supreme Court in connection with the cases involving segregation in the public schools, the Democratic United States Attorney General said: 'It is in the context of the present world struggle between freedom and tyranny that the problem of racial discrimination must be viewed . . . Racial discrimination furnishes grist for the Communist propaganda mills, and it raises doubt even among friendly nations as to the intensity of our devotion to the democratic faith.' He quoted the Secretary of State in his brief as saying: 'The segregation of school children on a racial basis is one of the practices in the United States which has been singled out for hostile foreign comment in the United Nations and elsewhere. Other peoples cannot understand how such a practice can exist in a country which professes to be a staunch supporter of freedom, justice, and democracy.' Within a few hours after the Supreme Courts' decision was read in 1954, the Voice of America had broadcast the news to foreign countries in thirty-five separate languages.

The establishment of the United Nations and the bringing of the headquarters of the organization to these shores suddenly threw open to the outside world a large window on American race practices. Through that window soon gazed a passing stream of delegates from all nations and races of the earth. To many of these people the Jim Crow code came as a complete shock. Those who had heard anything at all of the system before coming to America often discounted the stories as propaganda. Now they witnessed its workings daily. More important still were the United Nations committees of investigation, their numerous published reports, and the public debates that dealt with racial discrimination and injustice. The publicity thus focused upon this weak joint in America's moral armor caused genuine and practical embarrassment to the State Department in the conduct of foreign affairs. One of several stratagems employed to recover lost ground has been the appointment of numbers of Negroes to posts in the Foreign Service of the Department. Some of these posts have been of high rank and importance and have opened to Negroes a new access to prestige hitherto unattainable for them. National pride in the achievements of Ralph Bunche as an American spokesman illustrates the effect that the new prominence of the Negro in this field can have upon old prejudices and stereotypes.

There was concern in high office not only for the struggle over the allegiance of colored peoples in foreign lands but also for the allegiance of our own colored people at home. This was especially true with regard to the Negro intellectuals and the Negro labor leaders. Communist propaganda made a strong, powerfully organized, and concerted—if somewhat blundering—drive to alienate the Negro from his faith in American institutions, to destroy his hope for justice under segregation, and to win over his allegiance to the revolutionary cause. The effect this campaign had may be detected in the Negro periodicals, literature, and pronouncements of the 'thirties and 'forties, as well as among Negro leaders in cultural, intellectual, and labor fields. That the Communists failed was due only in part to their blundering. It was also due to a counter drive to revive the Negro's hope for a larger share in American democracy.

Among the chief agents for the advance against racial discrimination and segregation has been the federal government in its several branches and departments, both civil and military. The advances in leveling some of the distinctive barriers in Southern states could never have come so rapidly and effectively had not the powers and functions of the federal government undergone an unprecedented expansion during the last two decades. This expansion has been felt not only as an increase in power but also as an extension of that power into relations of employment, welfare, education, housing, and travel, where it had never before penetrated. In part the result of the crisis of the Great Depression, the enlargement of government functions and power was also a product of the same forces that have produced the oppressive wave of conformity—international tension, intensified nationalism, and war, both hot and cold.

4

The attack that led to the downfall of the old order in race relations had many preliminaries, as we have seen, but after the Second World War it moved into an accelerated phase the pace and radicalism of which would

justify calling it a 'Second Reconstruction.' This historic
movement falls into two fairly distinctive periods divided by the Supreme Court's decisions of 1954 and 1955
on segregation in public schools. In the first period the
executive and judicial branches of the federal government took the initiative in inaugurating reform, while
Congress and public opinion remained largely unre-
sponsive. In the second period, which will be treated in
the next chapter, massive Southern resistance challenged
the whole movement. Civil rights groups responded with
direct action that eventually aroused popular support
and stirred Congress into unprecedented and effective
action.

President Harry Truman was not without precedents
for executive action in behalf of Negro rights, for Franklin and Eleanor Roosevelt deserve credit for pioneer
roles. The New Deal was preoccupied with problems of
depression and war, however, and moved circumspectly
in the dealing with racial injustice and civil rights.
Roosevelt's first direct commitment, his executive order
of June 1941 establishing a Fair Employment Practices
Committee to supervise all defense-contract industries,
was made under threat of a massive demonstration, but
it set an important precedent.

It was Harry Truman nevertheless who broke through
the old bipartisan consensus on racial policy. In 1946 he
created a Commission on Higher Education, which reported the following year that 'there will be no fundamental correction of the total condition until segregation
legislation is repealed.' At the same time Truman ap-

pointed a Committee on Civil Rights that brought forth an uncompromising report entitled *To Secure These Rights,* calling for the 'elimination of segregation, based on race, color, creed, or national origin, from American life.'

In the face of a revolt that eventually took four states of the lower South out of his party, Truman in February 1948 urged the enactment of an F.E.P.C. law, the outlawing of poll tax and lynching, the elimination of segregation in interstate transportation, a law to enforce fairness in elections, and the establishment of a permanent civil-rights commission. In the same year the President issued an executive order to end discrimination in federal employment, and a momentous order to end segregation in the armed services.

A few minor cracks had been made in the wall of military segregation during the Second World War, but at the end of the war the old system was almost completely intact. In 1946, however, the navy, which had segregated the mass of Negro personnel in the messman's corps, began integration, as did the newly reorganized air force soon afterward. With a greater number and a larger proportion of Negroes than the other branches, the army showed more resistance to the idea. Then on 26 July 1948 President Truman issued an executive order 'that there shall be equality of treatment and opportunity for all persons in the armed services without regard to race, color, religion or national origin.' Generals and admirals, many of them convinced that it would not work and fearful of public reaction, nevertheless took their orders and kept news of the revolution from the press. Congressmen entered the conspiracy of silence, so that the full impact of the new policy did not become generally known until 1953.

In May 1950 the President received reports that in the navy 'Negroes in general service are completely integrated with whites in basic training, technical schools, on the job, in messes and sleeping quarters, ashore and afloat.' The air force had integrated about three-fourths of all Negroes in 1,301 mixed Negro-white units and had opened all its schools and jobs to both races without discrimination. The army lagged behind until the crisis of the Korean war, which began in the summer of 1950. With a surplus of Negro troops behind the lines and a critical shortage of white troops, who were bearing the brunt of casualties, one regimental commander in Korea explained that the 'force of circumstances' compelled him to integrate surplus Negroes into his decimated white platoons. It worked. The Negroes fought better than they had before. Race relations took a turn for the better instead of for the worse as feared.

Tested under fire, the new policy was rapidly applied to occupation and garrison troops in Austria, Germany, Japan, and throughout the many lands and continents in which American troops were stationed. The integration policy was also pushed forward at home. It was applied with no diminution or concession in the great army training camps in the Carolinas and Georgia, at the air bases in Alabama and Texas, at the naval bases in Virginia and Florida. It involved Negroes giving orders to whites, as well as whites to Negroes. It was extended to civilian employees as well as enlisted personnel, to living quarters of officers' families as well as to schools for their children. It did not stop at sleeping and eating arrangements, at bars, clubs, athletic fields, or swimming pools.

For the full impact of the results one needs the picture supplied by Lee Nichols of a barracks at Fort Jackson, South Carolina, where 'busily cleaning their rifles, Negroes from Mississippi and Arkansas sat on double-decker bunks among whites from Georgia and South Carolina with no apparent antipathy.' The long-range significance of the new military policy extended far beyond the limits of the armed services. Hundreds of thousands of men discharged from the services entered civilian life with an experience that very few, whether Northerners or Southerners, would have ever duplicated elsewhere.

President Truman also made efforts to implement his civil rights program in housing, fair employment practices, and other areas, but in none of these fields did he enjoy anything approaching the success of his attack on racial discrimination in the military services. White House leadership in the struggle for civil rights declined in importance in the administration of President Dwight D. Eisenhower. The most impressive achievement of the first Eisenhower administration in this field was in the capital city itself. Still thoroughly segregated in 1952, Washington underwent extensive desegregation in the next three years. Administrative action also ended segregation in Southern navy yards and in forty-seven veterans' hospitals. Beyond the range of direct federal authority, however, where there was federal-state conflict, Presidential leadership was withdrawn or silent. President Eisenhower's inactivity was in line with two often expressed principles of his philosophy of government. One was a preference for state over federal action: 'certain things are not best handled by punitive or compulsory federal law.' The other was a doubt, strongly reminiscent of the laissez-faire doctrine of William Graham Sumner, that any law could be effective in this area: 'I don't believe,' he said, 'you can change the hearts of men with laws or decisions.'

5

The real initiative and leadership in the early phases of the Second Reconstruction came neither from the executive nor the legislative branches, but from the federal judiciary. There was historical irony in the new role of the Supreme Court, for in the First Reconstruction it was the Court that had taken the role of reaction, restraining, frustrating, or destroying the radical advances in civil rights made by the executive and legislative branches. By narrow and ingenious interpretation its decisions over a period of years had whittled away a great part of the authority presumably given the government for protection of civil rights. Now in the new era the Court took the lead in reversing this trend and calling for ever greater exercise of federal power—greater often than the President or the Congress were willing or ready to assume, or the American voters were yet ready to support. So wide were the ramifications of the Court's decisions that it is possible here only to survey the more significant and typical results.

Because of its historic interest as one of the earliest areas in which the Jim Crow lawmakers entered, and because the Jim Crow car became the very symbol of the system, segregated transportation deserves special notice. The Supreme Court followed a course it took in other fields by first sharpening its insistence on equality of accommodations in allegedly 'separate but equal' facilities, and then eventually ruled out segregation itself. The early decisions were concerned with interstate, not intrastate, commerce. Not until 1946 did the Court, in *Morgan* v. *Virginia,* throw out a state law requiring segregation of a carrier crossing state lines. Four years later came a ruling against segregation on railway diners. Intrastate carriers remained untouched for a time and Jim Crow continued to prevail there. For lack of federal legislation, which Eisenhower was reluctant to demand, interstate carriers often continued for years after the Court decision to practice discrimination. Victory over segregation on trains and other carriers had to await the radical phase of the Second Reconstruction.

Another entrenchment of Jim Crow, older in the North than in the South, was residential segregation. The courts had struck much earlier at housing segregation by law, but the practice continued under the protection of private restrictive covenants written into deeds and agreements. In 1948 the Supreme Court held these private agreements invalid on the ground that they deprived minorities of equal protection of the laws. The decision made relatively little impression on the actual structure of segregated housing, however, and effective reform had to await more radical and vigorous action.

Disfranchisement measures adopted around the turn of the century had excluded all but a tiny percentage of the Negroes from the polls in the Southern states for nearly half a century. Efforts to abolish the poll tax by federal law were repeatedly defeated, and though several states did abolish the tax, literacy tests and intimidation kept Negro registration at a minimum. Even those registered could be disfranchised by the white primary, the most formidable barrier of all. Beginning in 1941 with the *Classic* case, the Supreme Court reversed previous decisions upholding the white primary and pronounced it unconstitutional. Evasive measures, including efforts to convert the Democratic party into a private club, were repeatedly struck down. Recognizing the primary as the real election in the South of that day, the Court refused in subsequent decisions, including one in 1953, to uphold any party rules excluding the Negro on the ground that the delegation of this authority by the state 'may make the party's action the action of the State.'

As a result of these decisions and other forces, Negroes began to return to the polls of the South. A study sponsored by the Southern Regional Council indicates that in 1940 only about 2 per cent of the total number of Negroes of voting age in twelve Southern states actually qualified to vote. By 1947 some 12 per cent, or more than

600,000 were so qualified, and by 1952 some 1,200,000. For the first time since the beginning of the century Negroes reappeared in elective and appointive office, largely in the upper South, on school boards, city councils, and other minor posts. 'Sixteen major Southern cities,' according to a study made in 1953, 'employ nearly 65,000 Negro persons, and 468 of these are engaged in managerial or professional tasks.'

In the lower South, apart from a very few cities, however, little change in Negro voting or office-holding could be detected. By one means or another, including intimidation and terror, Negroes were effectively prevented from registering even when they had the courage to try. After 1954 and the rise of militant Southern resistance, Negro registration slowed down and for a time actually declined. In many Black Belt counties it was apparent that so long as voter registration and poll supervision were entrusted entirely to local authority there would be little hope for significant Negro participation in the most elementary political rights.

In their struggle for justice in the courts, as in their fight for the ballot, Negroes were also aided by a friendly Supreme Court. In a series of decisions, beginning in 1939, the Court repeatedly ordered new trials for Negro defendants on the ground that members of their race had been systematically barred from jury service in the counties where the trial took place. As a consequence Negroes slowly reappeared on juries and grand juries in some parts of the South, though their chances for equal treatment and justice continued to suffer from grave handicaps.

Efforts of civil-rights groups to secure passage of a federal anti-lynching law failed repeatedly, but effective work by white and Negro groups, many of them Southern church organizations, virtually eliminated lynching for a time. The N.A.A.C.P. conceded 'the virtual disappearance of this form of oppression' in the early 1950's. It was to reappear later with the rise of Southern resistance to civil rights campaigns in the Deep South. Before the resistance mounted its reaction around 1955, Southern liberal efforts for civil rights were not wholly ineffective. Six states adopted laws, aimed at regulating the Ku Klux Klan, prohibiting the wearing of masks and the burning of crosses. Forty-odd private universities and colleges admitted Negro students without legal compulsion. A few cities began to open public libraries, parks, and museums on a non-segregated basis. Negro news began to receive fairer treatment in Southern newspapers. Private organizations, with church-affiliated activities leading, began to abandon the color line voluntarily. Some of the professional associations, learned societies, lawyers, nurses, librarians, and social workers followed suit. Not all the reform was the consequence of outside pressure, and it would be unfair to the South and unfaithful to the facts to leave that impression. But the margin of activity for Southern liberals and moderates was never broad, and it was to narrow sharply with the rise of militant Southern resistance.

Before that set in, universities and colleges, particularly the professional schools, made considerable progress toward integration. Negroes seeking admission relied on the 'equal protection' clause. The Supreme Court responded with several decisions that increasingly broadened the definition of 'equality' and increasingly found 'separation' incompatible with it. A Missouri case in 1938, involving Negro admission to a state school, indicated that the Court would insist upon the provision of equal training opportunities, regardless of how few Negroes applied for them. But two cases cracked the wall of segregation in higher education. In *Sweatt* v. *Painter,* a Texas case, the Court ruled in 1949 that a hastily established law school for Negroes did not meet the standard of equality because of 'those qualities which are incapable of objective measurement but which make for the greatness in a law school.' The following year, in *McLaurin* v. *Oklahoma,* the Court ruled that even though a graduate student was admitted to the University of Oklahoma for instruction, he did not enjoy the equality guaranteed by the Fourteenth Amendment so long as he was segregated within the classroom, the cafeteria, and the library. 'Such restrictions,' held the Court, 'impair and inhibit his ability to study, engage in discussions and exchange views with other students, and, in general, to learn his profession.' That would seem to have outlawed segregation in publicly supported higher education.

And so for the first time, except for abortive experiments in the First Reconstruction, Negro students appeared with white students at Southern state institutions.

By the fall of 1953 they were enrolled in twenty-three publicly supported colleges in Southern or border states at the graduate level, and in ten at the undergraduate level. All this had been done without violence or serious resistance, but it was done on a token basis and before an uglier mood of defiance had developed. No integration had yet taken place in five states of the lower South. When their turn came a less favorable temper prevailed.

In the public schools the rule of Jim Crow remained complete and unbroken throughout the Southern states and in several states beyond. Segregation was required by law in the schools of seventeen states and the District of Columbia, permitted by local option in four, prohibited by law in sixteen, and eleven states had no laws on the subject. In the South it was increasingly apparent from the Supreme Court's ever-stiffening standards of 'equality' that if the public schools were to operate under the old rule of 'separate but equal,' they would have to be equal in fact as well as in theory. They were very far from that in most respects, and in many areas Negro schools were disgracefully behind schools for whites.

Acknowledging that time was running out, Governor James F. Byrnes of South Carolina admitted that 'To meet this situation we are forced to do now what we should have been doing for the last fifty years.' The question was whether the injustice of half a century or more could be repaired before the courts would close forever the separate-but-equal loophole for segregation. The chances were slight at best, but several states began a desperate attempt at equalizing Negro schools. Thirteen

Southern states spent about eight times as much for school construction and maintenance in 1951-52 as they had in 1939-40. They were attempting the impossible task of maintaining two equal school systems with the lowest per-capita income of any part of the country. While they narrowed some gaps, the disparities between white and Negro education continued to yawn wide in many areas. Before the equalization had proceeded very far, the Court was seriously debating whether completely equal schools for the two races could be constitutional so long as they were completely separate.

In the meantime the Supreme Court had been moving cautiously and deliberately toward a momentous decision. Five cases challenging the constitutionality of segregation in schools had been moving up slowly from South Carolina, Virginia, Kansas, Delaware, and the District of Columbia. Represented by dedicated and able attorneys of the N.A.A.C.P. in all but one case, the plaintiffs were attacking not merely inequality but segregation itself. After a hearing in December 1952, the Court ordered the litigants to submit briefs on an elaborate list of questions for a new hearing a year later of the case now known as *Oliver Brown et al.* v. *Board of Education of Topeka, Kansas.* Never had the Court moved more deliberately. All arguments were having their day in court.

On 17 May 1954 the new Chief Justice Earl Warren delivered the unanimous opinion of the Court in favor of the Negro plaintiffs. Dismissing the historical argument regarding the intentions of the framers of the Four-

teenth Amendment toward segregation in schools as 'inconclusive,' the opinion held that history could give no
adequate answer. 'We cannot turn the clock back to 1868
when the amendment was adopted,' held the Court, 'or
even to 1896 when *Plessy* v. *Ferguson* was written. We
must consider public education in the light of its full
development and its present place in American life.'
Under these circumstances, 'Segregation of white and
colored children in public schools has a detrimental effect upon the colored children,' for it 'generates a feeling of inferiority as to their status in the community that
may affect their hearts and minds in a way unlikely ever
to be undone.' At this point the opinion cited in a foot-
note writings of social scientists supporting this view.
'We conclude,' said the Chief Justice, 'that in the field of
public education the doctrine of "separate but equal"
has no place. Separate educational facilities are inher-
ently unequal.' The plaintiffs had therefore been 'deprived of the equal protection of the laws guaranteed by
the Fourteenth Amendment,' and consequently segregation in public schools was unconstitutional. The Court
then ordered still further argument on problems of implementing its decision, thus virtually postponing the
issue for a year.

The Court's decision of 17 May was the most momentous and far-reaching of the century in civil rights. It reversed a constitutional trend started long before *Plessy*
v. *Ferguson,* and it marked the beginning of the end of
Jim Crow. But the end was to be agonizingly slow in
coming.

V

The Declining Years of Jim Crow

For all the finality of the Court's decision on a principle of fundamental importance, there was at the time an air of unreality about the revolutionary implications. Public opinion outside of the South was receptive and generally favorable to the departure, but by no means aroused to the point of stern insistence on compliance. Certainly the Administration in Washington was in no mood to adopt heroic measures that would be required for enforcement. Negro leadership was actively engaged and hopefully alert to problems of implementing the decision, but the mass of Negroes had not yet been stirred by the possibilities it opened nor aroused to the pitch of protest and demonstration. All these considerations had their effect on the way in which the South responded.

1

For a time after the decision of 17 May 1954, there
appeared to be grounds for optimism. The Court's precedent breaking opinion seemed to destroy all legal
foundations for segregation. Yet there were no sensational outbursts of defiance. The restrained tone of the
Southern press and Southern leaders was the subject of
wide comment and congratulations. The comment of
the Nashville *Tennessean* on the day following the decision was not unique: 'It is not going to bring overnight
revolution,' said the editorial, 'but the South is and has
been for years a land of change. Its people—of both races—
have learned to live with change. They can learn to live
with this one. Given a reasonable amount of time and
understanding, they will.' None of the old-style demagogues of the sort who had commanded several states a
few years back were presently on hand to make capital
of the issue. Scattered localities in the border states announced their intention to abolish segregation in the
schools, and Washington and Baltimore moved ahead toward that objective with exemplary speed. The late Professor Howard W. Odum of the University of North
Carolina, an authority on race relations, went so far as
to predict that 'the South is likely to surprise itself and
the nation and do an excellent job of readjustment.'

In view of the adjustments or readjustments the South
had already made in race relations over the preceding

decade, Professor Odum's prediction did not seem unreasonable. Southern white people had adjusted to the return of the Negroes to the polls in several states, to their appearance on juries, school boards, and white-collar jobs, and to their admission to colleges and universities. The whites had 'moved over' in some degree to make room for colored Southerners in various professional associations, collegiate and professional athletic teams, in dining cars, and Pullman cars. Southern white draftees drilled, ate, and shared barracks with Negro draftees in all the military services, and took orders from commissioned and noncommissioned officers of both races. To each successive stage the South had adjusted peacefully, if often grudgingly.

Surveying all these changes in established Southern practices, changes few thought they would live to see, men of good will began to entertain hopeful expectations about the future. The Jim Crow system still stood, but its foundations had been shaken. Segregation was on the defensive; in some quarters it was in retreat. If all this had been accomplished without bloodshed, reasoned the optimists, perhaps a new day had really dawned. Perhaps the South might eventually take the transition to unsegregated public schools in its stride as well.

There followed a year of marking time until the Supreme Court handed down its decree of implementation, which was not to come until May 1955. In the meantime neither side showed its hand fully. There was neither any appreciable progress toward desegregation in the schools, save in the border states, nor did the segregationists yet mobilize for all-out resistance. It was a period of wait-and-see.

A few signs appeared to indicate what was to come. Mississippi came forward in her historic role as leader of reaction in race policy, just as she had in 1875 to overthrow Reconstruction and in 1890 to disfranchise the Negro. The third 'Mississippi Plan' took the form of the Citizens Councils, which were started at Indianola in July 1954, to wage unremitting war in defense of segregation. Balancing these negative developments, however, voices counseling compliance and moderation continued to be lifted in the South, even in parts of the Deep South. On the whole, during the year that followed the original Supreme Court decision on public school segregation there was remarkably little of the hysteria that was to develop in the South later.

The spell was not even broken by the Supreme Court's decree of 31 May 1955 implementing the decision against segregated schools. The decree was actually greeted by some in the South with expressions of relief and even hailed as signifying the Court's acquiescence in indefinite postponement of desegregation. Indeed, the Court had set no deadline for compliance. It had referred sympathetically to the 'solution of varied local school problems' which would require time; it placed the responsibility for solving these problems upon local school authorities, and it charged the federal district courts with the duty of passing upon 'good faith implementation.'

More than anything else, it was the reference to the district judges and 'their proximity to local conditions' that raised the hopes of segregationists. The old four-handed American game between the South, the courts, the Negro, and the Constitution had been going on throughout our history, and the South knew all the moves. For much the greater part of that period, the courts had played into the hands of the South and the game had gone against the Negro. If now the Supreme Court had changed partners, the South could still place its hopes in the district judges, many of whom were natives of the states in which they sat. This hope was most explicitly voiced by Lieutenant Governor Ernest Vandiver of Georgia, who rejoiced that 'they are steeped in the same traditions that I am. . . . A "reasonable time" can be construed as one year or two hundred. . . . Thank God we've got good Federal judges.'

While the judges ground out their answer in the months that followed the Supreme Court's decree, the segregationists watched with growing disappointment and dismay. By January 1956, nineteen court decisions involving school segregation cases had been rendered, and in every one of them the lower courts upheld the Supreme Court ruling that enforced segregation was a denial of equal protection of the law. While some of the decisions took a lenient view of the amount of time required to desegregate, others stressed the 'prompt and reasonable start' required by the Supreme Court's directive and set dates for compliance. School segregation laws were toppled in Florida, Arkansas, Tennessee, and

Texas. On 15 February, Federal District Judge J. Skelly Wright, New Orleans-born and educated, smashed Louisiana's plan to preserve segregation in schools through state laws. Judge Wright admitted all the terrible difficulties involved in desegregation, as well as the need for 'the utmost patience, understanding, generosity and forbearance' on the part of all. 'But the magnitude of the problem may not nullify the principle,' he declared in a ringing conclusion. 'And that principle is that we are, all of us, freeborn Americans, with a right to make our way unfettered by sanctions imposed by man because of the work of God.'

On top of these blows from quarters where comfort had been expected, came attacks from the Negroes themselves. No longer the familiar, submissive creatures whom white Southerners thought they knew and understood so well, Negroes had begun to realize that they at last had the law and the courts on their side. It could no longer be pretended that they were indifferent to the issue. They were ready to assert their rights more forthrightly than they had for three generations. In the summer of 1955 the N.A.A.C.P. filed petitions for desegregation signed by local Negroes with 170 school boards in seventeen states.

2

Something very much like a panic seized many parts of the South toward the beginning of 1956, a panic bred of insecurity and fear. Race relations deteriorated in many areas, and as both races recoiled, old lines of communication between them snapped or weakened. On the white side, resistance hardened up and down the line, and in places stiffened into bristling defiance. The Citizens Councils movement spread out from Mississippi into Louisiana, Alabama, Texas, Arkansas, Florida, and Georgia. A national official of the organization in New Orleans claimed a membership of 500,000 members in eleven states. As a result of their activities, signers of desegregation petitions in Mississippi, in Selma, Alabama, and in Orangeburg, South Carolina, were fired from their jobs and refused credit by stores and banks so as to compel them to withdraw their names. Negroes brought to bear economic weapons of their own, most notably in the bus boycott in Montgomery. There were individual cases of violence against N.A.A.C.P. members and at least one murder. On 6 February 1956 occurred the first instance of violence in connection with the admission of a Negro student to a formerly all-white college or university—after more than a thousand cases of such admission in the South. This was the riot on the campus of the University of Alabama over the admission of Miss Autherine Lucy.

The long-feared and long-predicted reaction in the South was at last under way and gaining ground rapidly. In the first shock of apprehension, in genuine fear of more explosions in chain reaction, Southern liberals and moderates raised the cry of forbearance, directed toward the North. Further pressure and haste at the moment, they maintained, would leave them no ground on which to stand and would only provoke additional violence that would defeat the purposes of the reformers. The appeal met with wide response among Northern liberals, many of whom called for an easing of the pressure and a slowing down of the campaign against segregation.

The initiative, however, had already passed over to the reaction. Leadership of the reaction was not limited to disreputable hate groups and rural demagogues. The State of Virginia, usually a seat of moderation and conservatism, lent all her great prestige of leadership in historic crises of the South to the side of reaction. It was Senator Harry F. Byrd who called upon the South for 'massive resistance'; and it was the conservative leaders of his state who claimed the right of 'interposition' of state authority against alleged violation of the Constitution by the Supreme Court, and who pointed the way toward the private-school plan as a means of evading the Court's decision and preserving segregation. In the first three months of 1956 the legislatures of five Southern states—Alabama, Georgia, Mississippi, South Carolina, and Virginia—adopted at least forty-two pro-segregation measures, mainly dealing with schools. Many other measures were pending, and by July twelve new segregation bills had been approved by the Louisiana legislature.

Virginia's interposition plan, or some variation of it, was taken over by all six of the states mentioned in the previous paragraph. Alabama was the first actually to apply the fateful words, 'null, void, and of no effect' to the Supreme Court school decision. The resolution was endorsed by a voice vote in the Senate and an 86 to 4 vote in the House. Georgia also adopted the 'null and void' approach, adding a strongly worded declaration that it intended to ignore the Supreme Court decision. Mississippi declared the decision 'unconstitutional and of no lawful effect,' and created a State Sovereignty Committee 'to prohibit . . . compliance with the integration decisions.' Avoiding the word 'nullification,' South Carolina contented herself with 'condemnation of and protest against the illegal encroachment of the central government.' The Louisiana legislature adopted its interposition resolution without a single negative vote in either house. The North Carolina legislature defeated interposition but adopted a 'resolution of protest' against the Supreme Court decision.

In addition to these more or less rhetorical gestures of defiance, four states bluntly proclaimed a policy of open resistance by imposing sanctions and penalties against compliance with the Supreme Court's decision. The Louisiana legislature would withhold approval and funds from 'any school violating the segregation provision' of its laws. Georgia made it a 'felony for any school official of the state or any municipal or county schools to spend tax money for public schools in which the races are mixed.' North Carolina would also deny funds to local authorities who integrated their schools, and Mississippi made it unlawful for the races to attend publicly supported schools together at the high school level or below. Both Mississippi and Louisiana amended their constitution to provide that to promote public health and morals their schools be operated separately for white and Negro children.

Such undisguised defiance as these measures represent was more significant as a barometer of popular resentment than as an effective legal defense of segregated schools. Probably in the same category, though somewhat more serious as an obstacle to integration, belong the various state plans for evading desegregation by substituting some form of private education for the public schools. These plans were analogous to those by which South Carolina sought to evade the Supreme Court's ruling against the white primary a few years back by converting the political party into a private organization and claiming the state had no control over its primary elections. This method applied to education had no more prospect of success before the courts than it did as applied to primaries. This did not prevent several states from resorting to the device. Mississippi and South Carolina amended their constitutions to enable their legislatures, counties, or school districts to abolish the public schools, and Georgia entertained a similar amendment. Alabama provided permissive legislation enabling the state and its subdivisions to discontinue public schools and turn over public money to aid private education. Georgia and North Carolina would make grants to parents of school-age children to be used in paying private tuition. These measures were accompanied in some states by various provisions for leasing or selling of school buildings and property to private individuals.

Few of their authors could have expected such laws to stand the test of the courts very long.

More serious as obstacles to the progress of desegregation were the numerous new regulations governing assignment and attendance of pupils. They were generally designed to create administrative obstacles to legal action and tie up and string out litigation so as to discourage efforts at integration. A key device of this sort was the transfer of all authority over assignment and enrollment of pupils to local authorities. This would make it necessary to sue each local authority individually and thereby slow down the pace of litigation. In framing the new rules governing assignment of pupils, the lawmakers invoked the police power of the state 'to preserve the peace, protect the health, and morals . . . and insure the peace, health, contentment, happiness, and tranquility to all the people of the state,' as Tennessee put it. Virginia would take into account 'personality, practices, needs and desires; the intensity of racial feeling'; and Georgia authorized local superintendents to consider sociological and psychological data in assigning pupils.

It is unnecessary to labor the possibilities of resistance, evasion, and delay opened by laws of this sort. 'There is no one way, but many,' as John Temple Graves of Alabama pointed out. 'The South proposes to use all of them that make for resistance. The decision tortured the Constitution—the South will torture the decision.' The Court ruled against segregation on grounds of race or color only—not against segregation on grounds of health, morals, illegitimate birth, public welfare and tranquility. On grounds comparable to these the Negro was for half a century denied the ballot that the Fifteenth Amendment plainly said he could not be denied on grounds of race or color. And when those possibilities are exhausted, there still remain token compliance accompanied by real evasion and all the devices of *de facto* segregation which were effectively and quietly used in other parts of the country without any legal support at all.

As yet there were no 'teeth' in the Court's decision against segregated schools. That is, there were no sanctions such as the Civil Rights Act gave to the Fourteenth Amendment for a time during Reconstruction, or the Volstead Act gave to the Eighteenth Amendment. State laws could gradually be brought to test before the courts. But there were thousands of local school boards in the segregating states to which the ball could be passed by the state, and they in turn could invent new troubles for the courts.

Progress toward desegregation of public schools during the two and a half years that followed the Supreme Court decision was not impressive, and it was largely confined to the border states and the District of Columbia. The school year 1956-57 opened in the seventeen Southern and border states with 723 school districts and school units desegregated, a gain of 186 over the previous year. Of those districts that had any Negro pupils, some 3000 remained segregated. In all, approximately 300,000 Negro pupils were in 'integrated situations,' though not necessarily going to school with whites, and about 2,400,-

000 were entirely segregated. Two schools in Tennessee, three school districts in Arkansas, and more than a hundred school districts in western Texas were desegregated. But in the eight states of Alabama, Florida, Georgia, Louisiana, Mississippi, North Carolina, South Carolina, and Virginia the rule of segregation in the lower school level remained unbroken.

For a time it seemed as if the policy of defiance or determined resistance would be followed by only five or six states. The border states gave early indication of compliance, and the so-called mid-South states—Tennessee, Arkansas, Texas, and Florida—appeared to be inclining toward the example of the border states rather than in the opposite direction. From the first, however, heavy pressure was brought to bear upon moderates or waverers to line up with resistance. Proponents of the Southern 'Declaration of Constitutional Principles,' issued on 12 March 1956, were able to get the signatures of all the congressmen from seven states, and 101 of the 128 members from eleven states. Among the signers were several political leaders who had previously spoken in tones of moderation and from whom better leadership was expected. Yet the manifesto deplored the Supreme Court's 'clear abuse of judicial powers' and commended 'the motives of those states which have declared the intention to resist forced integration by any lawful means.'

In the spring of 1956 the school segregation issue figured prominently in seven state primary elections. Two North Carolina congressmen who refused to sign the Southern manifesto against the Supreme Court went down to defeat. Governor James E. Folsom of Alabama became a major casualty of the segregation issue by losing almost three-to-one to a pro-segregationist in a race for election as Democratic national committeeman. The policy of resistance spread southward into Florida, westward into Arkansas, and northward into Tennessee. Under the leadership of Governor LeRoy Collins, Florida had professed an official policy of gradual acceptance of integration. In March 1956, however, Governor Collins declared that 'we are just as determined as any Southern state to maintain segregation.' In the same month Governor Orval Faubus of Arkansas, where there had already been a small start at integration, took a stand for segregation that won the praise of the executive secretary of White America, Inc. The governors of North Carolina and Texas announced strong support for new segregation laws in their states. During the summer of 1956 the legislatures of Florida, North Carolina, and Virginia were called into special sessions to consider bills designed to tighten segregation laws. By the end of the year eleven Southern states had placed a total of 106 pro-segregation measures on their law books. When the public schools opened in the fall, flurries of violence broke out in Tennessee, Texas, Kentucky, and West Virginia as mobs sought to block the admission of Negro pupils in some of the first Southern schools to be desegregated.

It is probable that some of this defiance can be attributed to political excitement in an election year. On the other hand it was clear that the law of the land as defined by the Supreme Court had been defied and that the defiance had the support of responsible spokesmen for millions of Americans.

3

Given the temper of the times in the country at large and the mood of the Eisenhower Administration, the prospects for the success of resistance in the South were not at all bad. President Eisenhower refrained from any expression of approval of the Supreme Court decision and for more than three years he failed to speak out for compliance. He repeated his thought that 'you cannot change people's hearts merely by law.' In February 1956 when the Supreme Court ordered the University of Alabama to admit its first Negro student, Autherine Lucy, for graduate study, violent mobs menaced the student while she was attending classes and the trustees of the University suspended her for her own safety and 'the safety of the students and faculty members.' When a federal district judge on February 29 ordered the University to reinstate Miss Lucy, the trustees 'permanently expelled' her the same day for making 'outrageous' charges against them. Eisenhower said, 'I would certainly hope that we could avoid any interference.' The federal government did nothing, and the University of Alabama continued segregated for seven more years.

President Eisenhower was not the only political figure of importance to take a noncommittal stand on segregation. Both the Democratic and the Republican national conventions of 1956 debated the public school desegregation in a timorous and gingerly way and adopted vacuous planks on the subject for their platforms. The Republican platform declared that the party 'accepts the situation' (the classic formula of the defeated Confederates in 1865), and the Democratic platform said the decision had 'consequences of vast importance.' The Democratic nominee, Adlai Stevenson, told a Negro group that 'We must proceed gradually, not upsetting habits or traditions that are older than the Republic.'

The country was clearly in no mood for radicalism. It was only beginning to emerge from a shattering crusade against radicals and a paranoid intolerance of any opinion to the left of Senator Joseph McCarthy. The electorate had made it evident in many ways that it had had enough of reformers and government interference with private affairs, and that it yearned for political tranquility and uninterrupted opportunity to enjoy the fruits and pleasures of affluence. The only area of affairs in which the government (more specifically the judicial branch) dared challenge the prevailing mood was the area of race relations. This gave the exception a geographical boundary as well, for race problems were then regarded as largely a Southern peculiarity.

These circumstances recall those of the First Reconstruction, which was conducted in a period described as the Gilded Age. It was also a postwar era that, after a few years of peace, had had enough of idealism, self-sacrifice, and crusades and was exuberantly preoccupied with material things and self-indulgence. The electorate had placed in the White House a popular general who was celebrated for qualities other than moral enthusiasm. Political leaders of the period, unusually cynical about politics and lax in public morality, nevertheless found themselves saddled with a mandatory program of heroic idealism and revolutionary change in race relations for the South that was quite out of tune with the predominant temper in both North and South. The Grant Administration gave nominal support to the program and under pressure even intervened with military force at times to restore order and uphold federal law. But the support was half-hearted and lacking in conviction, and the Southern resistance triumphed over federal law and brought the First Reconstruction down in ruins.

But there were many differences between the two instances. In the First Reconstruction the South was severely handicapped by a crushing defeat, military occupation, partial white disfranchisement, and total Negro enfranchisement. The resistance in the second instance suffered under no such handicaps. It was powerfully represented in Congress itself, occupying strategic seats of federal power, frustrating efforts of enforcement, intimidating friends of the law, and recruiting Northern support of resistance.

All over the South the lights of reason and tolerance and moderation began to go out under the resistance demand for conformity. During 1957, 1958, and 1959 a fever of rebellion and a malaise of fear spread over the region. Books were banned, libraries were purged, newspapers were slanted, magazines disappeared from stands, television programs were withheld, films were excluded.

Teachers, preachers, and college professors were questioned, harassed, and many were driven from their positions or fled the South. The N.A.A.C.P. was virtually driven underground in some states. Words began to shift their significance and lose their common meaning. A 'moderate' became a man who dared open his mouth, an 'extremist' one who favored eventual compliance with the law, and 'compliance' took on the connotations of treason. Politicians who had once spoken for moderation began to vie with each other in defiance of the government.

Governor Orval E. Faubus of Arkansas had been elected over an all-out segregationist and had earned a reputation for moderation. Arkansas had already accepted some token school integration. But in September 1957 Governor Faubus called out national guardsmen to prevent nine Negro students from entering the all-white Central High School of Little Rock. He withdrew the guardsmen on court order, and three weeks later the nine children entered the school. At this point a huge waiting mob, hysterical, shrieking, and belligerent, defied police and forced the removal of the Negro children. Whereupon President Eisenhower, who had said two months earlier that he could not 'imagine any set of circumstances that would ever induce me to send federal troops,' ordered one thousand paratroopers to Little Rock and placed 10,000 Arkansas national guardsmen on federal service. The children returned to school and the troops remained on guard the rest of the year. But the rebellion was not over. In its most important decision since 1954, and in much sterner tones, the Supreme Court in September 1958 firmly and peremptorily refused to permit a postponement of integration because of the violence. Faubus then closed the high schools of Little Rock and declared, 'I will never open the public schools as integrated institutions.' The schools remained closed throughout the school year 1958-59.

Faubus became a regional hero as waves of sympathy for him spread over the South. The Governor was returned to office for an unprecedented third term by an unprecedented vote and continued to enjoy repeated reelections. Virginia, with a tradition of conservatism and a small Negro population, used her prestige in the South to head the defiance of law. Three Virginia cities closed their public schools to prevent integration in 1958 and attempted to improvise private segregated schools for the locked-out white children. Segregationists were jubilant and moderates were silent. Desegregation of public schools in the South came virtually to a halt. In the first three years after the *Brown* decision, 712 school districts were desegregated, but in the last three years of the Eisenhower Administration the number fell to 13 in 1958, 19 in 1959, and 17 in 1960.

In the meanwhile, Southern resistance to federal authority received aid and comfort from other parts of the country. The Supreme Court was under attack for reasons often not concerned with segregation and fell under criticism by learned and eminent authorities. In August 1958 the annual Conference of Chief Justices of State Supreme Courts voted by an overwhelming majority of

38 to 8 to demand that the United States Supreme Court exercise more self-restraint. In Congress the Court was subjected to assaults of explosive violence. The House passed bills restricting the Court's powers, and the Senate came within eight votes of nullifying several Supreme Court decisions and within one vote of prohibiting the Court from excluding states from any legislative area occupied by Congress unless that body specifically agreed. On top of this the President refused to deny a report that he privately deplored the *Brown* decision and said that integration should proceed more slowly.

Encouraged by these signals, resistance stiffened in the South. The lower South had given no signs of compliance whatever and openly boasted of the fact. Passive resistance and civil disobedience were old traditions in America, and their triumphs had not all been on the side of the angels. Traditional respect for the law had been overridden by the conviction of millions that the *Brown* decision and its sequels were not to be properly regarded as the law of the land. Thousands were persuaded by Citizens Council propaganda to believe that whole branches of the federal government had been taken over by conspiratorial and mainly foreign subversives.

4

Until 1960—in several ways a turning point—the Southern resistance had been able to persuade itself that the civil rights movement was wholly the result of 'outside agitators,' that Southern Negroes were contented and happy with the 'Southern way of life,' that they preferred segregation, and that left to themselves they would never think of protesting. It is true that the myth had received some jolts, most notably in 1955-56 by the year-long boycott of the city buses of Montgomery in protest against segregation. This completely successful demonstration was inspired and led by native Negroes and brought forth a leader of national stature in Dr. Martin Luther King, Jr., founder of the Southern Christian Leadership Conference (S.C.L.C.). The Montgomery boycott inspired similar demonstrations in other cities. But 1960 was the year of massive awakening for the Negroes of the South—indeed Negro Americans generally.

On 1 February of that year four Negro college boys, freshmen at the Agricultural and Technical College in Greensboro, North Carolina, asked politely for coffee at Woolworth's lunch counter and continued to sit in silent protest when refused. The 'sit-in,' nemesis of Jim Crow, was born. In a week it spread to six other cities of the state, and by the end of the month to seven other Southern states. The self-discipline and fortitude of the youths, who silently bore abuse and insult, touched the white South's respect for courage. A few Northern and Southern whites joined the demonstrators in parades and picket lines. In April the Student Nonviolent Co-ordinating Committee (S.N.C.C.), was formed—small, militant, very youthful, largely Negro, and Negro-led. The sit-in demonstrations gained momentum and power as they spread through the whole South and involved non-

violent direct action by thousands who had never protested before.

The Negro awakening of 1960 was more profound and
impressive than the abortive stirring of 1867. It was
deeper, surer, less contrived, more spontaneous. More
than a black revolt against whites, it was in part a gener-
ational rebellion, an uprising of youth against the older
generation, against the parental 'Uncle Toms' and their
inhibitions. It even took the N.A.A.C.P. and CORE
(Congress of Racial Equality) by surprise. Negroes were
in charge of their own movement now, and youth was in
the vanguard. Affected only slightly at first by the rising
tide of belligerence among colored races abroad, the
American movement was essentially indigenous. One of
the great uprisings of oppressed people in the twentieth
century, it could have taken an ominous form had it not
been for two extremely fortunate circumstances. One
was the *Brown* decision of 1954 that had prepared the
way for redress of grievances by constitutional means.
The other was that all the major civil rights organizations, new as well as old, were committed to the philosophy of non-violence, the doctrine preached by the most
conspicuous leader in the Negro movement, Martin
Luther King. 'We will soon wear you down by our ca-
pacity to suffer,' he told the whites, 'and in winning our
freedom we will so appeal to your heart and conscience
that we will win you in the process.' All but the most
incorrigible white resistance was vulnerable to such a
weapon.

The walls of segregation began to crumble under the

new assault. Lunch counters yielded in more than a hundred cities within a year. The sit-in tactics were broadened to attack segregation in theaters, hotels, public
parks, swimming pools, and beaches, as well as in
churches, courtrooms, libraries, and art galleries. Boy-
cotts supplemented sit-ins to deal with discrimination in
service or employment among merchants and other business establishments. Some disorder and rioting broke out
and thousands were jailed, but for more than a year
serious violence was minimal. Considering the masses
involved and the emotions aroused the record was remarkable. Violent recalcitrance was inevitable in the
hard-core white-supremacy states, however, and it came
with shocking explosiveness in May 1961 in reaction to
'freedom rides' sponsored by CORE to challenge segregation in interstate buses and terminals. At Anniston,
Alabama, a mob attacked riders and burned their bus.
White hoodlums attacked other riders at Birmingham,
and at Montgomery a mob beat a score of people in
several hours of rioting that had the apparent sympathy
of police and some city authorities. Federal marshals and
the Alabama National Guard were required to restore
order. Police prevented mob attacks on freedom riders
in Mississippi, but jailed more than three hundred and
gave some of them brutal treatment.

By this time a change had begun to overtake the complacency and conservatism that characterized the American temper in the 'fifties. The national conventions of
both major parties in 1960 adopted outspoken anti-segre-
gation planks for their platforms and expressed approval

of the sit-in demonstrations. The successful candidate, President John F. Kennedy, came to office with strong commitments to the Negro movement and obligations for Negro support of his candidacy. His inauguration brought a new era of federal recognition for Negro aspirations and the appointment of a number of Negroes to high office. The President's positive support for the *Brown* decision, which he pronounced 'both legally and morally right,' in his inaugural address, was soon manifest in new energies devoted to the enforcement of federal court orders for school desegregation.

Massive resistance began to collapse in all but the Deep South in the fall of 1959, when Little Rock reopened its schools on an integrated basis. A shift toward Southern compliance came in 1960 with the conviction that 'another Little Rock' must be avoided. In that year Houston, Raleigh, Knoxville, Richmond, and Roanoke admitted Negroes to their schools without disturbance, but ugly violence accompanied the process in New Orleans. Encouraged by Governor Jimmy H. Davis and the state legislature, whites boycotted the schools, and snarling, jeering mobs of pickets with uncontrolled fanatics in command exhibited to the world American racism in some of its more revolting aspects. The Supreme Court struck down Louisiana barriers to integration, which went forward the next fall. In 1961 Atlanta, Dallas, Memphis, Tampa, and Galveston desegregated their schools peacefully. In 1960 and 1961 the number of desegregated school districts in the old Confederate states rose from twenty-six to sixty, and by the end of the latter year only Alabama, Mississippi, and South Carolina had admitted no Negroes whatever. The first peaceful year of public-school desegregation, 1962 saw the number of Negro children in school with whites nearly doubled in seven states, yet this was all on a token, almost microscopic basis. At the end of the ninth year of 'deliberate speed' after the Supreme Court decision, fewer than 13,000 Negro public school pupils out of 2,803,882 were in school with Southern whites. It began to appear that compliance on a basis of 'tokenism' was evasion of the law and a perpetuation of segregation under the guise of compliance.

5

In Mississippi and Alabama resistance had hardened throughout these years, when neither state showed any sign of complying with the law of the land as interpreted by the Supreme Court. Mississippi, however, easily maintained its historic priority in racism. The state with the largest Negro minority and the last state to have a black majority of population, Mississippi was also the poorest state in the Union, and the most profoundly isolated from national life and opinion. Professor James W. Silver described it as 'a closed society,' which 'comes as near to approximating a police state as anything we have yet seen in America.' Its Negroes lived in constant fear and its whites under rigid conformity to dogmas of white supremacy as interpreted by a state-subsidized Citizens Council. In 1955 three Negroes were lynched, the first in the country since 1951, and one was a fourteen-year-old boy, Emmet Till. No one was punished, nor were any of the lynchers who took another victim in 1959. Less than 2 per cent of the Negroes over twenty were registered voters. Law enforcement was in the hands of bigots, and bigotry was respectable.

White Mississippians were totally unprepared in September 1962 to accept the federal court order by Justice Hugo L. Black to register James Meredith, a native Negro, as a student in the University at Oxford. They had been assured repeatedly by state courts, the state legislature, and Governor Ross Barnett that the sovereign state would prevent it and that integration was unconstitutional. On 24 September Barnett issued a proclamation directing that 'representatives of the federal government are to be summarily arrested and jailed' if they interfered with state officials. The Governor physically and personally blocked Meredith's registration on the 25th and Lieutenant-Governor Paul B. Johnson, on the 26th.

On Sunday afternoon 1 October a force of 320 federal marshals entered the university campus at Oxford and installed Meredith in a dormitory. That evening President Kennedy addressed Mississippians over a national television hook-up appealing to reason and patriotism and saying 'the honor of your university and the state are in the balance.' He was too late and the force he employed too little. The marshals were already under furious attack, first by students and then by much larger armed mobs from outside admitted by the state troopers that Barnett had at the last moment promised the President would be used to maintain order. This was not an attack on Negroes or demonstrators. It was an insurrectionary assault on officers and soldiers of the United States Government and the most serious challenge to the Union since the Civil War. The mob fought with stones, bricks, clubs, bottles, iron bars, gasoline bombs, and firearms. The besieged marshals, supplemented by federalized Mississippi national guardsmen and later by regular army troops, relied mainly on tear gas. The battle raged all night, and by dawn, when the troops routed the mob, two people had been killed and 375 injured, 166 of them marshals, 29 by gunshot wounds. The campus battlefield was littered with wrecked cars and trucks, tear-gas cannisters, and other debris. Meredith was then registered. Of the maximum commitment of 30,000 troops, three hundred remained until July 1963.

The year following the Battle of Oxford was full of violence in the lower South. The worst exploded in Birmingham, where as early as April 1960, according to *The News York Times,* 'Every channel of communication, every medium of mutual interest, every reasoned approach, every inch of middle ground [had] been fragmented by the emotional dynamite of racism, reinforced by the whip, the razor, the gun, the bomb, the torch, the club, the knife, the mob, the police and many branches of the state's apparatus.' The lines were drawn and no middle ground remained. The firebrand Governor George C. Wallace declared in his inaugural address in January 1963, 'I draw the line in the dust and toss the

gauntlet before the feet of tyranny and I say segregation
now, segregation tomorrow, segregation forever.'

In April the Reverend Fred Lee Shuttlesworth of
S.C.L.C., together with Dr. King and the Reverend
Ralph D. Abernathy, launched a campaign for limited
desegregation goals in Birmingham, which Negroes
called 'the Johannesburg of America.' Police Commis-
sioner Eugene 'Bull' Connor had closed all city parks,
playgrounds, and golf courses rather than submit to a
court order opening them to all citizens. He had been
defeated for Mayor on April 2, but was still in control.
Connor's police halted the sit-ins the first day by arrest-
ing some 150 demonstrators. King and his associates then
defied an injunction and staged a march and 'kneel-in'
on Good Friday. Connor arrested King, Shuttlesworth,
and Abernathy—the thirteenth arrest for Dr. King. The
demonstrations continued day after day, larger and
larger, packing prisons with marchers, hundreds of them
school children. On 2 May police arrested about five
hundred. The next day onlookers threw stones and bottles at police when they knocked down students by fire
hoses and attacked them with police dogs. With the situation threatening to get out of hand, Assistant Attorney
General Burke Marshall intervened at Birmingham and
with the help of personal pressure from the President
and cabinet members and national leaders of the business
community, negotiated a truce that suspended demonstrations on 8 May. City authorities promised the Negroes
fulfillment of basic demands in ninety days. Even before
the agreement was announced, Governor Wallace re-

pudiated it, declaring he would 'not be a party to any
. . . compromise on the issues of segregation.'

On the night of 11 May, after a meeting of the Ku
Klux Klan near Birmingham, two dynamite explosions
blasted the home of Dr. King's brother, and within an
hour two more bombs shook the headquarters of the
Negro movement, the Gaston Motel. Thousands of angry
Negroes surged into the streets and rioted out of control
for three hours, attacking and being attacked by police.
Two Negro homes were burned and four buildings, including a store, belonging to whites were put to flames.
Fifty people were hospitalized before the rioting was
stopped by state troopers. Three thousand federal troops
were sent to the area but did not have to be used. Dr.
King and others quieted rebellious spirits, promised no
further demonstrations, and pledged the Negroes to
abide by the agreement previously made with the city.

But Birmingham had become a symbol for an out-
raged people all over the country, and the pictures of
helpless Negroes attacked by police dogs and brutal police were flashed all over the world. National anger and
impatience with Alabama recalcitrance deepened when
a week after the riots a federal judge ordered the University of Alabama to admit two Negroes on 10 June,
and Governor Wallace replied defiantly that he would
'be present to bar the entrance of any Negro who attempts to enroll . . .' President Kennedy sternly warned
the Governor against defiance and made military prepa-
rations. Wallace nevertheless went through the motions
of 'standing in the schoolhouse door' before the tele-

vision cameras, but abandoned his contrived stage when the President federalized the Alabama National Guard.

Alabama had still not had its fill of melodrama, and the next act was not bloodless. Birmingham waited tensely for the integration of public schools ordered by a federal court for September. More violence broke out sporadically in the summer, but local officials were preparing for peaceful school integration. Suddenly on 2 September the Governor sealed off the schools with state troopers and placed national guardsmen at the doors in Birmingham and two other cities whose schools were to be integrated. President Kennedy promptly federalized the guard and ordered them to their barracks. Negro children entered the schools, and peace reigned—for five days.

The following Sunday morning at 10:25, just after Bible class ended at the Sixteenth Street Baptist Church, rallying place for demonstrations in the spring, a tremendous blast of dynamite smashed holes in the walls of the basement. Under the wreckage were found the lifeless bodies of four girls, three age fourteen and one eleven. Fourteen other Negroes were injured. Mobs poured into the streets and police dispersed them by firing over their heads. A policeman killed a sixteen-year-old boy with a shotgun fired from behind. A boy of thirteen was shot to death while riding a bicycle. Those guilty of the bombing, like those guilty of fifty previous bombings of Negro property in Birmingham, were never found or convicted. Charles Morgan, Jr., a young Birmingham lawyer, told his fellow white citizens his solution to the crime the very day after it occurred: 'The answer should be "We all did it." '

The Birmingham atrocities set off demonstrations over the whole country and deepened the impatience and anger of Negroes and their friends everywhere. A new martyr to the cause was added on 12 June by the murder of Medgar Evers, N.A.A.C.P. state secretary of Mississippi, shot from ambush in front of his home at Jackson. The man accused of the murder was freed after two mistrials. Interracial violence burst into flames at Cambridge, Maryland; Danville, Virginia; Lexington, North Carolina; Tallahassee, Florida; and Philadelphia, Pennsylvania. Large numbers of white church groups and college students were now involved in protests. In the ten weeks following the Birmingham truce and the Evers assassination, the Justice Department counted a national total of 758 racial demonstrations.

The greatest of all was a national demonstration, the March on Washington of 28 August, organized by A. Philip Randolph and Bayard Rustin. It assembled more than 200,000 people, the majority black but many white, before the Lincoln Memorial. It was the greatest demonstration for redress of grievances the capital had ever seen. The crowd was peaceful and good-natured, a 'sort of national high-water mark in mass decency,' according to the press, but no one could hear their response to Mahalia Jackson's song or Dr. King's lyrical address, 'I have a dream,' without sensing the profound emotions that were stirring in the crowd and in the millions who watched by television. Americans were now looking to the Federal Government for action, and the Kennedy Administration was keenly aware of the mood of the country.

Congress was already debating a new Civil Rights bill at the time of the March on Washington. Two such measures had been adopted in recent years. The Civil Rights Act of 1957 was concerned mainly with federal protection of voting rights for Negroes, but it originally contained a section giving power to the Justice Department to bring suit in behalf of any civil right, including voting and school desegregation. This crucial section was deleted under Southern attack. An outgrowth of this act, the Civil Rights bill of 1960 authorized judges to appoint referees to help Negroes register and vote and provided criminal penalties for bombing and mob action to obstruct court orders. Like the previous act the Civil Rights Act of 1960 was whittled down before adoption, and both measures proved a disappointment to civil rights leaders. The efforts of the Justice Department in behalf of Negro voting rights were not effective and demonstrated the need for stronger laws.

Early in 1963 President Kennedy had sent a relatively mild civil rights bill to Congress, but he admitted that 'the events in Birmingham and elsewhere' had drastically altered his sense of urgency. In the midst of those events, on 11 June he addressed the nation in the most powerful appeal for civil rights yet made by a President. 'The fires of frustration and discord are burning in every city, North and South,' he said. 'Where legal remedies are not at hand, redress is sought in the streets in demon-

strations, parades and protests, which create tensions
and threaten violence--and threaten lives.' Eight days
later he sent to Congress the most sweeping bill for civil
rights up to that time, and urged it 'not merely for reasons of economic efficiency, world diplomacy and domestic tranquility—but above all because it is right.'

The proposed legislation covered equal access to all
public accommodations, prohibited discrimination in
any state program receiving federal aid, outlawed racial
barriers in employment, in labor union membership,
and in voting, and authorized the Justice Department
to bring suits for desegregation of public schools. Only
a few months earlier many of these proposals would
have been considered unthinkable. But the President
moved with determination to build up support for
them in a series of White House meetings with leaders
of labor, business, professional, and women's organizations. He also threw his personal influence into the
effort for the necessary bipartisan backing of his bill.
By the time of his death on 22 November, President
Kennedy had completely committed his Administration
to civil rights and helped to evoke a national commitment to the same cause.

6

History had repeated itself—or rather a few familiar
lines of itself. For the second time the assassination of
a President had brought a Southerner to the White
House to preside over a reconstruction of race relations.

But there the repetitions ended. Between the two Southerners, the only two to hold the office for a century, there could not have been a greater contrast in the degree of commitment to the cause they inherited. Lyndon B. Johnson made the cause personally his own in a way no previous President had, embracing it with the passionate energy characteristic of the man. Within five days of taking the oath of office he demanded in a message to Congress that it give priority to 'the earliest possible passage of its Civil-rights bill.' Within the next week he called to the White House all of the prominent Negro leaders, one at a time. He then unfroze the blocked bill by pressure on Congressmen and addressed the nation in support of it. He would be content, he declared, with 'nothing less than the full assimilation of more than twenty million Negroes into American life.' Martin Luther King called the President's message 'a heroic and courageous affirmation of our democratic ideals.'

The struggle for the Civil Rights bill dragged out for seven months, delayed by every means, including more than five hundred amendments and a long filibuster, that its opponents could devise. The measure had the support not only of a determined President, but of a lobby consisting of thousands of clergymen and other supporters. Enactment finally came on 2 July, 1964, and President Johnson signed it the same evening. The ban on Jim Crow discrimination in hotels, motels, restaurants, theaters, and all places of public accommodation went into effect immediately. Instead of the 'wave of defiance' predicted in the South there was rather a wave of peaceful compliance, even in cities of the lower South, though not in rural areas. Jim Crow was mortally wounded but not entirely dead.

Civil rights was not the only issue in the Presidential election of 1964, but it was the most powerful issue. Johnson's opponent, Barry Goldwater, in savage attacks on the Civil Rights Act left no doubt about his stand. He expected support from the much predicted "back-lash'" vote of Northern whites and segregationist South. Riots broke out during July and August in New York, Rochester, Chicago, Philadelphia, and three New Jersey cities. They were not of the magnitude of riots to come in later years, but the looting and violence did augment the 'blacklash' vote. Nevertheless, Goldwater carried only the five states of the lower South plus Arizona, his own. On the other hand, in spite of a landslide victory, Johnson carried only one state of his native South, his own.

Violence in the North and the excitement of the election had temporarily diverted attention from the battle-front in the lower South. On 4 December, however, the F.B.I. arrested twenty-one Mississippians, including the sheriff of Neshoba County, in connection with the mur-der of the three young civil-rights workers. They had disappeared on 21 June, and their bodies were found on 4 August. The leering defiance of the sheriff and his men and the difficulties of the federal government in bringing them to justice brought home to the country the help-lessness of the voteless Negroes when the courts and law

enforcement were completely in the hands of their
enemies.

This atrocity was the worst of several in connection
with the Mississippi Summer Project, a campaign to
register Negro voters by SNCC, CORE, S.C.L.C., and
the N.A.A.C.P. banded together into a Council of Fede-
rated Organizations (C.O.F.O.). The project attracted
upward of a thousand 'outsiders' as volunteers, many of
them Northern white students. The kind of opposition
they encountered is suggested by casualty statistics: 1000
arrests, 35 shooting incidents, 30 buildings bombed, 35
churches burned, 80 people beaten, and at least six murdered. At this cost C.O.F.O. claimed to have aroused
Mississippi Negroes to political consciousness, developed
the Freedom Democratic party, awakened whites to their
responsibilities, and established native Negro leadership.
Only a handful of Negro voters were actually registered,
but the very ineffectuality of the registration campaign
strikingly demonstrated the need for powerful federal
aid that the law did not so far provide.

To dramatize further the difficulties that Negroes
faced in attempting to register and vote, civil rights
groups decided upon demonstrations in Selma, Alabama. Slightly more than half its population were
Negroes, yet they accounted for only one per cent of its
registered voters. For two months Negroes marched to
the courthouse to register and were stopped by Sheriff
Jim Clark, who jailed 2000 demonstrators. A state
trooper shot and killed Jimmie Lee Jackson, a Negro,
in a nearby town. Dr. King then called for a march of

fifty miles to Montgomery and defied Governor George Wallace's order forbidding it. On Sunday 7 March state troopers assaulted the marchers in a sickening attack with clubs, whips, and tear gas while a national audience watched in horror. The reaction was spontaneous and furious. Demonstrators took to the streets in scores of cities, and thousands, including 400 clergymen, poured into Selma to join the march to Montgomery. One of the clergymen died of a beating received in Selma.

The march was delayed pending the decision of a federal court, and then on 21 March it went forward under military protection ordered by President Johnson. Five days later on the outskirts of Montgomery the marchers were joined by 20,000 sympathizers from all parts of the country to complete the march through the streets of the city to a thundering climax before the Alabama state capitol. All went peacefully until that night when Ku Klux Klansmen murdered a woman demonstrator on the highway back to Selma.

In the midst of the Selma crisis and in response to the issues it raised, President Johnson summoned a joint session of Congress and addressed to its members and a national audience a stirring appeal to 'overcome the crippling legacy of bigotry and injustice.' His message included a powerful demand for federal protection of Negro voting rights. The President called for 'a law designed to eliminate illegal barriers to the right to vote' and 'provide for citizens to be registered by officials of the United States Government.' With bipartisan support a bill took shape during the next four months which set aside the literacy tests and authorized federal examiners to begin registering Negroes in Alabama, Georgia, Louisiana, Mississippi, South Carolina, Virginia, and 34 counties of North Carolina.

The Voting Rights Act, signed by the President on 6 August 1965, rounded out a year of unparalleled legislative achievement for civil rights. The year started with the monumental Civil Rights Act of July 1964, aimed at racial discrimination in public accommodations, public schools, housing, labor unions, employment, and economic opportunity. Some of the more important provisions of the 1964 Act were just going into effect while the finishing touches were being put on the Voting Rights bill. The Administration showed promptness and dispatch in implementing the new laws. Nothing comparable had ever happened before even during the high moments of the First Reconstruction. For then the three branches of the government were constantly at odds, and the states waged defiant resistance. This time President, Congress, and Court were in full harmony, and state resistance appeared to be crumbling.

For a very brief interval the optimists had things their way. At long last, they contended, American institutions were responding effectively to the most serious domestic problem the country faced. Jim Crow as a legal entity was dead. Congress had fulfilled its role, the courts were vindicated, and the executive furnished inspired leadership. Granted that discrimination and segregation still flourished in spite of the law, nevertheless the means were now at hand to deal with all these problems. A national consensus was in the making, and a peaceful solution was in sight.

In support of the more cheerful view of the future it could be pointed out that in absolute terms Negro Americans had scored more gains in the preceding two decades than in any period since emancipation. These gains were registered in saving accounts, insurance policies, and purchasing power; in high school and college diplomas and expanding opportunities for those qualified for professional and clerical jobs. The new status in politics was indicated by eight Negro federal judges, four United States ambassadors, the appointment of Thurgood Marshall as Solicitor General, and scores of other high-level federal appointments. Negro candidates captured more than 280 elective offices, including six seats in Congress and ninety-odd in state legislatures, several of them in the South. Optimists also pointed to the voting strength Negroes had gained by adding 450,000 voters in the Southern states within the year before the Voting Act was passed—nearly as many as they had added in the five preceding years. Now with the powerful new laws on the books, with public sentiment behind them, and an Administration thoroughly committed to the cause, a new era of progress was about to dawn. It was even predicted that Negro Americans could at last put behind them their old frustrations, bitterness, and despair and face the future with new hope and confidence.

A comparable mood of optimism and euphoria had

accompanied the legal end of slavery just a century before the legal end of Jim Crow. Both moods were natural
reactions to the end of long and costly crusades. But the
optimists in both instances shared two assumptions. The
first was that the legal end of the institution abolished
meant the end of abuse that was outlawed. The second
was that the institution abolished was responsible for
all, or nearly all, of the troubles of its victims. These
assumptions proved to be tragically fallacious, as those
who cherished them in both centuries were soon to
learn.

VI

The Career Becomes Stranger

Only five days after the signing of the Voting Rights Act, which marked the peak of optimism for the civil-rights movement, the country was shaken by a terrible explosion on the West Coast that ranked with the worst racial violence in American history. On 11 August 1965 a riot broke out in Watts, a Negro district of Los Angeles, and raged for four days unchecked and three days longer in sporadic convulsions. More than 46 square miles had to be brought under military control before the violence was halted. Thousands of blacks in bands looted stores, set fires, burned cars, and stoned and shot at police and firemen. At the end of it 34 people, all but three of them Negroes, were dead, more than 1000 injured, and nearly 4000 arrested. More than 600 buildings were damaged and a third of them completely destroyed by fire with property losses of about 40 million dollars.

1

The title of the official report on the Los Angeles
riots, *Violence in the City—An End or a Beginning?*
posed a question in 1965 for which history was soon to
provide a tragic answer. Watts was only a beginning. It
was not a cause but a precursor of events. For four
summers, 1965 through 1968, pictures of flaming cities,
looting and embattled mobs, and smoking ruins were
regular features of newspapers and television. In that
period more than 150 major riots and hundreds of minor
disturbances occurred in cities as diverse and scattered
as Los Angeles, New York, Cincinnati, Des Moines,
Tampa, Chicago, Atlanta, Milwaukee, Erie, Buffalo,
New Haven, Washington, Newark, and Detroit. The
worst of all and the bloodiest racial violence of the
twentieth century in America occurred in Detroit during July of 1967. A force of fifteen thousand, including
federal troops, was required to end the violence. When
it was over forty-three were dead and more than a
thousand were injured. More than 2700 businesses
were sacked and about half of them completely demol-
ished. Whole sections of the city, including homes,
were reduced to ruins, a total area of fourteen square
miles gutted by fire.

The new type of violence not only dwarfed the violence of the civil rights movement in the South, but
was wholly different in nature. The President's Advisory
Commission on Civil Disorders concluded that while no

riot was 'typical' in all respects, most of them shared certain traits. While 'racial in character; they were not *inter*racial.' They took place within Negro districts and typically attacked not white persons so much as symbols of white authority—especially policemen, firemen, and National Guardsmen—and white property. The most common grievance was abusive police practices, and the recurrent complaint was discrimination and a sense of powerlessness. The typical rioter was somewhat better off than the average black in his community. He had the support of a large percentage of his black neighbors, who felt that the riot was a form of protest and might be beneficial, even though Negroes were the main victims. In spite of their extremist rhetoric, rioters made no real attempt to subvert the social order but rather sought to gain access to its benefits or to punish white offenders against the black community.

The apparent paradox of these unprecedented outbursts of black violence, disorder, and frustration exploding just at the peak of optimism bred of the civil rights movement and national commitments for improvement so recently made by the federal government came as a profound shock to many whites. A common explanation was that the civil rights struggle in the South had both sensitized Northern Negroes to their grievances and reduced their tolerance of old injustices. It had simultaneously increased their levels of expectation and shortened their patience with a white establishment that could not or would not fulfill those expectations. Hope rather than despair bred rebellion. There was doubtless much to be said for the theory of 'relative deprivation' in this whole matter. Many of the black ghetto grievances had existed a long time without producing such violence. But there were substantive as well as psychological changes to be taken into account.

The black exodus from the South to Northern cities turned the balance of population in the 'sixties, so that for the first time in American history almost as many Negro Americans were living outside the old Confederate states as within. Urban whites of the North were faced with progress in the South accompanied by deterioration and retrogression of race relations in their own backyards. The slow retreat of *de jure* segregation in the South had been paralleled by a rapid advance of *de facto* segregation of residence and schools in the North. The increases of black population in Northern cities was accompanied by a panic of white retreat to the suburbs and an acceleration of urban decay, crime, and delinquency. In employment the Negro's relative position had been slipping continually behind the whites. Since 1951 the gap between the incomes of white and black workers had been widening. In 1964 automation was wiping out some 40,000 unskilled and semi-skilled jobs a week, and since blacks were disproportionately employed in such jobs they bore the brunt of technological displacement. The rate of unemployment among them ran twice or more than that among whites. None of these acute problems was essentially touched by the Civil Rights Act of 1964 or the Voting Rights Act of 1965.

Striking incongruities appeared between the needs and moods of the black ghetto and the goals and strategies of the civil rights crusade, as typified by the leadership of Martin Luther King, Jr., and voiced in his lyrical Dream. Northern blacks began to ask what their problems had to do with freedom rides, sit-ins, and lunchcounter integrations—or, for that matter, with the ideal of racial integration and assimilation in general. While they had been stirred by the March on Washington, thrilled by the heroism of Birmingham brothers, and moved by the drama of the Selma March, they could not see how such tactics were adaptable to the scene at Newark, Detroit, Chicago, or Harlem. Granted the effectiveness of such crusading strategies for limited goals, even granting that they finally toppled the formidable but hollow legal defenses of Jim Crow—what now? Now on the very eve of those triumphs the triumphs themselves suddenly appeared quaint and anachronistic. What had they been but the belated fulfillment, partial at that, of promises a century old, restitution of historic commitments? They evoked racial yearnings of the past, powerful nostalgias for simpler and more heroic days, not answers to immediate needs and future problems. What had for years been the slogan of the day, the last word in an ongoing crusade, the leadership all acknowledged suddenly seemed old, dated, the commitments of another generation.

Not all at once, but with swiftness unparalleled by other shifts in the history of Negro thought, a great change overwhelmed the movement in midcourse. In large part it was a change from a predominantly Southern to a predominantly Northern orientation, a fundamental shift from which numerous other changes followed—changes in leadership, followers, and coalitions, changes in priorities, goals, and aims, shifts in style and strategy and rhetoric, changes in the musical accompaniments and the very songs the people sang. A predominantly religious tone gave way to a secular emphasis: preachers still held on, but intellectuals became more prominent; whites disappeared from front ranks, and white paternalism in any department became anathema. Less was heard about civil rights and more about economic demands; less about integration and assimilation and more about liberation and separatism. Southern accents gave way to West Indian inflections and jive talk. Rhetoric exploded with violence: Burn, baby, burn! Militant non-violence veered toward violent resistance and militants experimented with sniping, shootouts, and guerrilla tactics. Black nationalism revived all its old forms and assumed many new guises, uniforms, and slogans.

Old ways, styles, and leaders did not disappear without a struggle. Martin Luther King strove to retain his role as mediator between radical and conservative wings of black protest. He tried valiantly to adapt his tactics of non-violent direct action to the streets of Chicago, but the experiment was inconclusive. He was cut down by an assassin on 4 April 1968, before he was able to find the way into the future for his followers. They rallied after his death for a last crusade, a 'Poor People's March' on Washington which ended in confusion, misery, and failure. The old impulses, goals, and yearnings remained, but new and quite different slogans and leaders now claimed popular attention.

2

'This is our basic conclusion,' reported the President's Commission on Civil Disorders in 1968: 'Our Nation is moving toward two societies, one black, one white— separate and unequal.' The Commission was reporting the failure of the civil rights movement to achieve racial integration and reconciliation—not abandoning those goals, nor despairing of them. The report deplored the persistence of segregation and 'the continuing polarization of the American community.' It did not accept them as inevitable, and certainly not as desirable. Already, however, there were Negro spokesmen in favor of separatism who rejected integration, reconciliation, and assimilation as desirable aims of the race, who in one degree or another favored the racial polarization of American society, 'two societies, one black, one white,' that the Commission Report of 1968 deplored. The advocates of separatism differed widely in the kind of separateness they wanted, the completeness demanded, and the extremes to which they would go to achieve it. But they agreed broadly in repudiating—some in part and some completely—the very ideal toward which the civil rights movement had been striving.

The separatist impulse infected and took over some

of the major national civil-rights organizations themselves and split them apart along racial lines. Explicitly
interracial from its origins in 1942, the Congress of Racial Equality became a major force in the civil rights
crusade twenty years later. CORE had pioneered in
freedom rides, desegregation and voter registration
drives and school integration, but disenchantment with
these activities set in during the mid-'sixties. 'Integration is a dirty word,' declared the black chairman of the
San Francisco chapter in 1965. White members had out-
numbered black members before that time, and whites
were contributing over 90 per cent of CORE funds, but
they were rapidly alienated by black separatism and
anti-white feelings. The 1967 convention of the organization deleted the word 'multiracial' from its constitution to 'let the world know the direction CORE is
going.' Floyd McKissick, national director at that time,
spoke of Negro Americans as a 'nation within a nation.'
His successor, the Jamaican Roy Innis, announced the
following year that CORE had become 'once and for all
. . . a Black Nationalist Organization' with 'separation'
as its goal. Integration, he declared, was 'as dead as a
doornail.' But in consequence the organization itself
had become moribund.

A second civil-rights organization to embrace black
separatism was SNCC. Like CORE it was thought to
be ranged on the left of the movement as a militant,
uncompromising, moralistic group, primarily concerned
with the problems of the poor and local black communities. Both organizations were impatient with the slow

pace of change. On the whole, however, SNCC members were more likely to be true believers and less given to pragmatism. They were also more youthful, more Southern, and more prone to fill their whole lives with the movement and to face real danger. SNCC was predominantly black and led by blacks from the start, but its primary fight was against segregation, its goal some sort of integration. Whites joined and participated and served on the staff. 'Black and white together' was still a stirring chorus to 'We Shall Overcome,' and the original inspiration of Martin Luther King still lingered.

Interracial trouble within SNCC had stirred during the Mississippi summer of 1964. Northern white student volunteers became the objects of suspicion and jealousy from black co-workers, and some of them suffered racial abuse and violence. Advocates of separatism and violence worked to subvert the traditional ways of the movement, but so long as John Lewis remained chairman, SNCC continued to be nominally committed to integration and non-violence. Greatly beloved, Lewis was a Southerner and a friend of King. Early in 1966, however, he was maneuvered out of the chairmanship and replaced by Stokeley Carmichael, a youth of Trinidad origins and Northern background. His first move was to convert SNCC into an all-black organization and then to identify it with his slogan, 'Black Power.' Carmichael at first denied that his ambiguous slogan should be equated with black racism or separatism, but his successive redefinitions of the concept veered more and more in that direction and on toward a license to hate, to violence, and to rage. He was quoted later as defining Black Power as 'a movement that will smash everything Western civilization has created.' His successor in 1967 was H. Rap Brown, a cruder racist who preached guerrilla warfare, advised Cambridge, Maryland, protesters to 'Burn this town down,' and Washington rioters in 1968 to do 'more shooting than looting.'

Older civil-rights organizations yielded little to separatism. Some of their leaders were reluctant to speak out against advocates of the doctrines they opposed for fear of profiting hostile whites. But in 1968 the organ of the N.A.A.C.P. condemned 'a reversal of the trend toward integration' and blasted 'extremists who are shrilly and insistently espousing apartheid; racism, including anti-Semitism; intimidation and violence.' Bayard Rustin never wavered from the doctrine that 'separate is not equal' and in the nature of things could never be. He found it 'a great irony' to see people of his race seeking to impose upon themselves the very conditions of separation and inequality against which black Americans have struggled since the era of Reconstruction.

The fact was that for all the publicity they received the various advocates of separatism for a long time attracted no more than a small minority of the black population to their way of thinking. Reliable polls in the late 1960's identified no more than 15 per cent of the Negroes as separatists, and usually the percentage was smaller. So long as he lived after establishing his preeminence, Martin Luther King remained the favored spokesman of 85 to 90 per cent of Negro Americans polled. Whether in matters of employment, housing, or schooling, the vast majority of them preferred integration to separation. In spite of changing styles of rhetoric and slogans, their goals remained unchanged— an equal but integrated place in American life. Confronted with rejection by the great mass of Negro people, black separatists and extremists undertook to dramatize their causes and act out their fantasies in some improbable places.

One such place was the predominantly white Northern university or college. These institutions had admitted an increasing, but still relatively small, number of black students. The students brought with them perfectly legitimate demands for formal courses in Afro-American history, culture, sociology, and art. In the midst of academic efforts to respond to this acknowledged need, black nationalists sought to seize complete control of the new Afro-American programs and convert Black Studies into Black Nationalist Studies. Their avowed purpose in some instances was to revolutionize the black students and train cadres of revolutionists. They usually demanded autonomous departments with power to hire and fire, dictate curriculum, grant degrees, and exclude white teachers and students. Their purpose was not to integrate but to segregate education in the name of black nationalism. They varied in doctrine and rhetoric, but many shared the conviction of Stokeley Carmichael that it was 'precisely the job of the black educator to train his people how to dismantle

America, how to destroy it.' Extremists resorted to violence on some campuses, among them those of San Francisco State, Antioch College, Wesleyan University, and Cornell. Administration officials of Cornell found themselves solemnly signing concessions surrounded by gun-bearing black students and members of the press. When the faculty refused to ratify the administrative capitulation, an ultimatum from a leader of the armed students gave the university 'three hours to live.' The faculty reversed itself. At the Los Angeles branch of the University of California, rival clans of black nationalists shot it out with each other for control of academic programs, leaving two dead.

3

The politics of black nationalism need concern us here only in so far as it shaped the history of segregation and integration. Nationalist movements have influenced and reflected the course of that history in the past and still do. They have emerged in periods of disappointed hopes and betrayed promises following periods of high hopes and expectations. They have sought psychological solutions for social and political problems. They often fulfilled in fantasy the wish to be rid of the white man and his society. Since reactionary elements in white society always entertain fantasies of getting rid of the black man, they have often given support and encouragement to black nationalists.

The oldest form of black nationalism, the back-to-

Africa movement, was, in fact, of white origin, and every black revival of it down to that of the Jamaican Marcus Garvey has attracted white encouragement. Nothing of such wide appeal as Garvey's movement excited has appeared since, but the decolonization of Africa and the emergence of many independent nations in the early 1960's revived deep interest in the mother continent among Afro-Americans. The back-to-Africa aspect of that interest, after discouraging experiments, had begun to decline by 1965, though most black nationalists continued to voice the impulse in nebulous forms. Seceding and dissident nationalists, some fleeing the law and some the wrath of black opponents, took refuge in Africa as exiles and used it as a platform from which to hurl anathema at rivals and enemies back home. The most common form the African identification took was essentially non-political, a passing popular fashion of so called 'cultural nationalism.' Its African aspect found expression in the adoption of African names and the wearing of what were conceived to be typical African costumes and symbolic adornments. Hair styles proclaimed the conviction that Black is Beautiful. Other manifestations included the study of the African heritage, the search for elusive African survivals in American speech, custom, and art, and the study of African languages, folklore, and history.

Africa was by no means the only inspiration of black nationalism or the only source of its ideals and heroes. Identification of some sort was sought with the Third World generally. Solutions were found or imagined that

originated in Mecca, or Algeria, or Delhi, in Moscow, or
Havana, or Peking. Exotic heroes of other lands and
revolutions found homage, if doubtful comprehension
—Gandhi, Mao Tse-tung, Ché Guevara, Castro, Fanon.
It was not that their American admirers necessarily
adopted their philosophy, but that, as Bayard Rustin
put it, in their frustration and despair they were 'convinced that the only thing left to do is to give everybody
hell, to denounce everybody, and to call for revolt.' As
the authors of *Black Rage* described the mood in 1968:
'No more patience. No more thought. No more reason.
Only a welling tide risen out of all those terrible years
of grief, now a tidal wave of fury and rage, and all
black, black as night.' It would be folly to expect much
in the way of consistency or logic in expressions of such
a mood. Black nationalism had no 'party line,' no real
party. What its varied spokesmen had in common was
an antipathy toward 'integration' and 'nonviolence'—
the two ideals that the civil rights movement had shared.
Some of the new nationalists had once shared those
ideals themselves.

Not so Malcolm X. He was hard-bitten from the start,
and a youth spent in the underworld of crime and
prison had not softened him. He attributed his salva-
tion to the cult of Black Muslims to which he was
converted in jail and remained loyal until near the end
of his thirty-nine years of life. As a minister of that
faith he preached a gospel of puritanical abstinence,
hard work, racial purity and pride, and total racial separation. Integration was a fraud and the white man a

devil. Malcolm X was beyond doubt the most powerful
voice and easily the most impressive and brilliant leader
of the nationalist revival of the 1960's. In addition to
his followers, he commanded an interracial and an international audience. All manner of black nationalists
stood in awe of him. After his assassination in 1965 he
was virtually canonized, and competing separatist and
nationalist factions claimed his mantle. Most of them,
however, chose to ignore his break with the Black Muslims and his perplexed and uncompleted struggle in the
last year of his life to redefine his revolutionary goals.
He avoided in that period the use of the phrase 'black
nationalism,' renounced his racial chauvinism, and
looked forward to 'a society in which there could exist
honest white-black brotherhood.'

Prison was the school of black nationalists, for
younger men as it had been for Malcolm X. They
started out in the South, moved to California, fell into
crime, and landed in prison. This was the path followed by the three major figures in the short history
of the Black Panther party. Huey P. Newton was born
in Louisiana, the son of a black Baptist preacher, who
named him for his political hero, Senator Huey P. Long.
Eldridge Cleaver sprang from obscure origins in Arkansas, and Bobby Seale was the son of a Texas carpenter.
Newton took to robbing and pimping, Cleaver to rape
as 'an insurrectionary act.' In their youth they all fell
under Black Muslim influence for a time and hailed
Malcolm X as their hero. 'I have, so to speak, washed
my hands in the blood of the martyr, Malcolm X,' wrote

Cleaver. The urge to martyrdom was strong in him, as it was in his friends. He yearned for 'a bullet through the brain from the gun of the beleaguered oppressor on the night of the siege.' Huey Newton entitled one of his books *To Die for the People* and another *Revolutionary Suicide*. The rhetoric of violence took lurid and apocalyptic color in the pronouncements of the young revolutionaries. Newton headed a chapter on the founding of his party with a quotation exalting 'rage—black rage, apocalyptic and final.'

At first there was little to distinguish the Panthers from scores of black nationalist bands spawned in urban ghettos during the summers of riots. After an unpromising start in Oakland in 1966, they attracted Cleaver and later three leaders of a defunct SNCC, Carmichael, Rap Brown, and James Forman. None of these were to remain fixed in allegiance in spite of exalted office and title—Carmichael as successively 'Field Marshal' and 'Prime Minister.' Newton remained the dominant figure, even from prison. His 'Platform and Program' made numerous abstract demands for justice, the most explicitly nationalist being one of the vaguest, 'a United Nations-supervised plebiscite' for 'determining the will of the Black people as to their national destiny.' The issue with which the Panthers became most widely identified, however, was that of 'defending our Black community from racist police oppression and brutality.' For that purpose they required, declared Newton, 'the basic tool of liberation: the gun.' Guns in hand, they invaded the galleries of the California State Assembly while it was in session. Newton went to prison as the result of a shoot-out at Oakland in 1967 in which he was wounded and one policeman was killed and another wounded.

Always in flux, spinning from one irreconcilable ideology to another, the Panthers under Newton sought to combine a black vs. white race war of nationalism, black solidarity of all classes, with a 'Marxist-Leninist' class war in coalition with white revolutionaries. Carmichael, Forman, and Brown withdrew in bitter rejection of 'collusion with whites,' and Cleaver defected for other reasons. With Newton and Seale in prison and Carmichael and Cleaver in 'exile' by 1970, 'the Party was in a shambles,' according to Newton. Not only had the shoot-out and the gun become their symbols, but members had resorted to terror, torture, and murder against their own people. The Panthers, Newton admitted in 1973, had alienated the black people, 'defected from the community,' and become 'too radical to be a part of it.'

Such groups as the Panthers—never more than five thousand and probably not half that number, or the RAMS, Revolutionary Armed Movement, which was even smaller—would never have gained the attention and influence they did had it not been for the susceptibility of white upper-class Northerners. Unlike their Southern cousins, Northern whites had little experience and no tradition of dealing with guilt, and their experiments bordered on the bizarre and descended to the pathological. Many begged to be abused and baited.

Church dignitaries, law faculties, and foundation staffs sat submissively through barrages of abuse, 'confrontations,' that at least broadened their vocabulary of obscenities. Black revolutionary celebrities of the moment were sought as guests on Park Avenue and for country house weekends. Grave savants of Cambridge 'rapped' with them in staged 'dialogues.' Students of the oldest Ivy League colleges gathered at mass demonstrations in their support and embraced them as heroes. Churchmen tempered guilt with prudence and delivered only a small fraction of the three billion dollars in 'reparations' demanded by James Forman. Bankers, with fewer guilt problems and more prudence, delivered even less of the six billion demanded by Roy Innis. For some Yankees, however, guilt temporarily got the better of prudence, and at times it was a question whether it was guilt or cowardice that prevailed.

No doubt the style and rhetoric and violence of the black revolutionaries were 'too radical,' as Newton perceived, to be acceptable to the mass of black people. But the net effect and objective results were, as they had been for previous black nationalist movements, the opposite of radical. 'The irony of the revolutionary rhetoric in behalf of Negroes,' as Bayard Rustin observed, 'is that it has helped in fact to promote conservatism.' It provided emotional release for radical energies, substituted symbolic victories for the achievement of radical social goals, and further alienated the white working class with whom coalition would be essential for genuine radical politics. The myth of black

unity obscured the special interest of the black bour-
geoisie as beneficiaries of racial separatism. 'Black
power,' it has been pointed out, usually means black
middle-class power. Negro entrepreneurs, teachers, and
professional people, the educated and privileged class,
had acquired such status as it enjoyed in a segregated
society. E. Franklin Frazier called it 'a privileged status
within the isolated Negro community.' That status was
threatened by the removal of the legal foundations of
segregation. The ironically 'deprived' class stood to
gain benefits from racial unity, separatism, and black
nationalism. Some middle-class blacks, to be sure, sacrificed self-interest to serve the less fortunate. Left intact,
however, the black ghetto served as a kind of tariff wall
to protect a monopolized market.

Perfectly legitimate reasons would be found for expanding black enterprise, and there were genuine needs
for black participation in the administration of black
communities. But the great majority of black people
are not capitalists and like most whites probably never
will be, and the benefits of 'buying black' were more
those of the seller than the buyer. The idea attracted
support of corporate interests and the blessings of President Nixon. It cost little and left the ghetto to solve
its own problems. For black workers to define their
problem primarily in terms of race was to ally themselves with white capitalists against white workers. That
was the strategy of Booker Washington and Marcus Garvey. As the latter put it, 'The only convenient friend of
the Negro worker or laborer in America at the present

time is the white capitalist.' Advocates of 'black community control' were not black workers but aspiring Negroes with an eye on administrative posts in public
office, schools, hospitals, and social services. Their success would gratify racial pride, but it left the community
with the same problems of poverty, unemployment, bad
housing, and inferior schools.

4

Much was heard in the 1960's, especially during the latter half of the decade and the early 1970's, about 'alienation.' It was usually described in political terms as a
phenomenon of the left and associated with protest
against racial injustice and the Vietnam War. In social
terms it was ascribed especially to youth, particularly
college students, and to black people. In all those quarters, alienation, disillusionment, and distrust of the 'system' were certainly prevalent. With much of it white
liberals and old New Deal coalition elements of the
Democratic party identified and sympathized. But they
were unable to perceive and, when they did, unable to
identify and sympathize with an entirely different and
even larger class of alienated people. These lined up on
the right rather than the left, and their alienation had
little to do with Vietnam. They were not all of one
class, but they were all white, and they included nearly
twice as many caught below the poverty level as there
were blacks in that plight. They felt their grievances
deeply, and by all measurements the poll-takers could

bring to bear they were found to be far more alienated than whites in general and much more alienated than blacks of their own economic level. Moreover, they were more pessimistic about their future than were blacks about theirs, a great majority of whom felt in 1966 that 'things are getting better.'

A fateful thing about many grievances of the alienated whites of the right was the number of those grievances they were able, rightly or wrongly, to associate with blacks. Unlike upper-class whites, who often sympathized with black aspirations, the alienated class resented such advances as blacks made, opposed government and philanthropic measures in their behalf, and denounced the tactics and especially the violence of the black movement. It was not *their* movement. None of this was for them. They were the neglected, the forgotten. They bitterly rejected President Johnson's War on Poverty as another handout to blacks. Whites who had recently arrived at middle-class status shared these views, and even better-off whites of the right joined them in associating riots and crime, drug abuse and welfare increases, school and neighborhood deterioration, and the whole law-and-order issue with race. Their outlook was therefore thoroughly racist. The implications for the future of race relations and for the Second Reconstruction were ominous.

The foundations of the Second Reconstruction had, in fact, began to crumble during the Johnson Administration. By 1966 it had run a course since 1954 as long as the First Reconstruction had run from 1865 to 1877

and repeated some of its phases—from high fevers of
idealism, through achievement won by self-sacrifice,
and on through self-doubt, disenchantment, and withdrawal. Signs of the final phase, reaction, had set in.
White allies fell silent and cut contributions. Jewish
supporters were offended by the anti-Semitism of black
extremists, others by black separatism, racism, riots, and
hate slogans. White liberals and students became preoccupied with the Vietnam War issue. Labor leaders and
politicians became concerned with their 'image.' Negro
leaders were divided in counsel and their followers confused. Federal agencies charged with enforcement of
the sweeping provisions of the new civil-rights acts suddenly found their appropriations jeopardized, their
guidelines attacked, their orders brushed aside, and
their officers demoralized. Efforts to pass a new civil-
rights bill in 1968 languished for lack of support. 'The
trouble is that no one really cares any more,' said one
of its supporters. 'Crime in the streets,' he added, 'seems
to have replaced civil rights as the popular political
cause.'

In the meantime the dissaffected whites of the right
had found a champion of national appeal in Governor
George C. Wallace of Alabama. Known first as the leading defender of 'Segregation Forever,' he had broadened his appeal to 'little people' as their spokesman
against 'theorists' and others 'who look down their noses
at the street worker and the paper worker and the communications worker and the beautician and the barber
and the policeman and the fireman and the clerk and

the farmer.' Wallace had proved his drawing power for Northern voters in three primaries of the 1964 campaign, and in 1968 his name appeared on the ballot in all fifty states. His campaign thrived on heckling and demonstrations from the left. He was telling his people that their government had sold them out. His strength in opinion polls soared, and he threatened to carry enough electoral votes to throw the election into the House. Alarmed politicians of both the old parties trimmed to the right. The shift of the center of national politics that was to be completed in 1972 had begun. In 1968 Richard M. Nixon won with a slight plurality over Hubert H. Humphrey, who was still identified with the civil rights cause.

The new administration promptly applied brakes to federal spending for the advancement of black people. 'It is time,' said President Nixon in a State of the Union address, 'for those who make massive demands on society to make minimal demands on themselves.' He called for time out, time for hysteria to cool, time to appease the South, to placate alienated whites all over the country. In pursuit of his Southern strategy he nominated conservatives from that region for the Supreme Court and gave other signals that the tide had turned. He kept black Congressmen waiting many months for a reply to their request for an audience. The President smiled upon advocates of black capitalism, but sought to dilute the Voting Rights Act and preferred to go slow on desegregation. A Presidential adviser called it 'a period of "benign neglect" ' of the race issue. But the chairman of the N.A.A.C.P. convention in 1970 called it 'the first time since 1920 that a national administration had made it a matter of calculated policy to work against the needs and aspirations' of the black minority. On the other hand, the President did move with vigor when his hand was forced by the Supreme Court against the remaining defenses of *de jure* school segregation in the South.

The explosions of racial violence in the cities of the North had, since 1965, diverted national attention from the South. There had been relatively little violence in the South compared with the North, but deliberate resistance had slowed and stalled school desegregation. In October 1969 the Supreme Court ruled that persistent school segregation must be ended 'at once.' Only then, fifteen years after the *Brown* decision, did speed become more than deliberate. In fact desegregation moved with remarkable swiftness and, in spite of some trouble, with surprising smoothness. Progress in 1970 was impressive, and in 1971 the percentage of blacks in school with whites more than doubled in the South. By 1972 in the Southern and border states 44 per cent of the black pupils attended majority white schools. The schools of the South were now more desegregated than those of the North, where less than 30 per cent of the black children were in majority white schools. Boston, for example, found its public school system was more tightly segregated than that of any Southern city of importance below Washington.

Segregation in the North was no less real for being

de facto instead of *de jure,* but it was different in origin and more difficult to counter. Like that of the South it was the consequence of race prejudice, but it was the prejudice of individuals, not the act of the state or local government that was responsible for residential segregation which gave rise to the segregated schools. The massive flight of white city dwellers to all-white suburbs had added greatly to existing residential segregation and thus to the separation of school children by race. Should the courts move to correct 'racial imbalance' in Northern city schools by 'busing' children in and out of segregated residential areas and suburbs, as they seemed likely to do, they would touch the rawest nerve in politics. The desegregation issue would be transferred from South to North in an election year. As the President's chief civil-rights adviser pointed out, 'busing goes beyond schools and segregation—to all those other areas where people feel threatened in seniority, prestige, identity and begin to ask what are those bastards doing to us?'

In anticipation, Nixon declared in March 1970 for the principle of 'an "open" society' which 'does not have to be homogeneous, or even fully integrated,' and where 'it is natural and right that we have Italian or Irish or Negro or Norwegian neighborhoods.' Two years later, when a federal judge in Richmond handed down the anticipated decision ordering busing from adjacent counties to redress racial imbalance in city schools, Nixon was prepared. A constitutional amendment against busing was already before Congress, and Governor Wallace had made busing his leading issue in another Presidential campaign. In a message to Congress in March 1972, Nixon proclaimed the issue his own. 'I am opposed to busing for the purpose of achieving racial balance in our schools,' he declared and claimed that 'most Americans—white and black—share that view.' He added bluntly: 'But what we need now is not just speaking out against more busing, we need action to stop it.' After Wallace was eliminated from the Presidential race by a deranged gunman, the issue was indeed Nixon's own. The black vote did not respond, but white blue-collar workers, Catholics, and other ethnic voters did. Wallace voters in the South went for Nixon three to one and in the North six to five. Among the many meanings of the election of 1972, one seemed to be an end to the crusade against Jim Crowism.

5

After two decades of that crusade, both the crusaders and their opponents were divided among themselves over what it had accomplished, over the future of integration, and over the prospects and plans for black people in American society. Some were inclined to stress the substantial economic gains scored by Negroes during the 1960's and to discount habitual liberal rhetoric of failure as well as liberal battle-cries for renewed crusades. A few went so far as to call these gains 'revolutionary.' Gains there had been, and many of them were due to liberal measures—and liberals might indeed have done well to leave it to conservatives to point out the failures in their program. It was perverse and short-sighted of them to deny massive progress of the 1960's that blacks had scored in income, employment, education, and status. The claim that a little over half of the black population had crossed the line into the middle class seemed exaggerated, but at least 30 per cent had done so, as compared with barely 10 per cent in 1960. All these gains, of course, still left blacks as a whole far behind economic parity with whites and left millions of blacks in poverty. There were, moreover, signs that the gains of the 1960's were eroding in the 1970's. While the ratio of black to white unemployment had improved briefly, it had returned to the two-to-one level by 1973, and the number of blacks below the poverty line had risen to 33 per cent as compared with 9 per cent of whites. For all that, the economic gains for black people exceeded those of any other period in their history.

Political gains speak somewhat more directly than economic gains to the question of integration. Here there should be no question about the direct responsibility of old civil-rights movements for most of the accumulated gains. The Voting Rights Act of 1965, the government measures taken to enforce it, and the hard work of organizations and individuals account for the massive registration of Negro voters that made a breakthrough possible. Black voters were still intimidated in parts of the South, and turnout was often discouraging in many parts of the country, but gains in terms of offices held were undeniable. Black Representatives in Congress increased from five in 1960 to fifteen in 1972 (two from the South, the first since 1901), the number of black mayors from twenty-nine in 1968 to a hundred or more in 1973, the black delegations in state legislatures from 94 in 1964 to 206 in 1972, and the number of elective officeholders increased to 2600 by 1973, half of them in the South. None of these figures, of course, reflected in offices held the proportion of blacks in the population, but they did reflect a new order of black involvement and acceptance in American politics.

While black strivings and achievements in both the economic and the political field would seem to indicate on the whole more impulses toward integration than withdrawal and segregation of blacks in American life, the indications are not always clear. The struggle over the schools, once so clearly integrationist in purpose, became increasingly confused in both purpose and result. So long as school desegregation was considered a 'Southern problem,' the heat was on, and we have seen the striking progress made under pressure in the Southern states. Once it appeared that the courts were going to move against *de facto* school segregation in Northern cities, however, the commitment to integration quickly cooled. Many of the old Southern arguments re-emerged, this time from Northern mouths, those of liberals included: desegregation promoted racial conflict and disorder in schools; it was of doubtful benefit to black students anyway and many blacks did not want it; it destroyed neighborhood schools and neighborhoods; it was impossible in cities with growing black majorities in schools without busing, and that was too costly, counter-productive, and politically disastrous. It was doubtful how long segregation would flourish in the South if it proved the only region of which it was required. Cities there faced the same dilemmas and discouragements encountered in the North, and whites responded in much the same way. Those who were able to do so often withdrew to suburbs or private schools. If this continued, desegregation might become a condition largely confined to the poor and to rural people.

As white resistance to integration increased in the North, blacks listened more readily to the arguments of black separatists. They were demanding 'decentralization' and 'community control,' black school boards, black administration and black teachers to foster racial pride, black culture, and mutual respect. It was a voluntary retreat to 'separate but equal,' and it attracted much white support. Southern blacks, on the other hand, were slower to yield to separatism. Their experience with 'separate but equal' was longer and more bitter, and their investment in the crusade against it deeper and more passionate. In 1970, Dr. Benjamin Mays, black president of the Atlanta School Board, said, 'We certainly should not give up our efforts at integration and call it a failure.' Julian Bond, a young Negro legislator of Georgia, agreed that 'integration is still a viable goal, particularly in the South.' And Charles Evers, Mayor of Fayette, declared, 'It's beginning to work in Mississippi. It's going to work because we're going to make it work.'

By the 1970's confidence and principle were retreating before pragmatism and compromise. The new direction was pointed by Atlanta, whose schools were already 80 per cent black. The Atlanta chapter of the N.A.A.C.P., headed by Lonnie King, Jr., once a leader of student sit-in integration, worked out a compromise with white politicians that settled a fifteen-year-old integration suit by conceding that two-thirds of the city's 151 schools would remain virtually all black in exchange for a majority of the top positions. in the system for black administrators. The Second Atlanta Compromise attracted wide attention and inspired imitation. Integrationists feared that it might become the way of the future and the ultimate betrayal of their cause.

The struggle between integrationists and separatists continued unabated, however, and on many fronts. In its tortuous course the debate suggested that the career of Jim Crow might become even stranger than it had been in the past. Black champions of separatism joined hands with white champions of segregation. Former integrationists accepted separatism as the viable compromise. Was a new 'capitulation to racism' under way? Some voiced that suspicion. 'Is *"Plessy* vs. *Ferguson"* really coming back? I think that possibility exists,' said Vernon Jordan, head of the National Urban League. 'The issue is: are we today going back to separate and unequal?' Southerners were inclined to agree with Charles Evers that 'You can't have equal and separate.

Somebody is going to get the short end.' The N.A.A.C.P. saw itself with some exaggeration as 'the last civil rights organization that still believes in integration.' Yet it was also still the largest and oldest of them. The national office painfully suspended the officers of its strong Atlanta branch because it believed that the Second Atlanta Compromise, like the First, sacrificed principles to promote middle-class jobs and interests in a new black exclusionism.

Even separatists and nationalists admitted that in terms of mass support black integrationists still exceeded nationalists, and opinion polls continued to sustain that view. Yet many circumstances made it increasingly difficult to answer some of the separatists' questions: How do we integrate with whites constantly in flight? How many will the exodus to suburbs leave us to integrate with? Are the cynics not right who define 'integration' as the period between the time the first Negroes move in and the last whites move out? Is the quality and control of schools not more important than their integration? How can we argue with the brute facts of demography? Instead of undertaking an impossible 'breaking up the ghetto,' why not consolidate it as a base of power and position? Is integration worth the risk of accepting white values to the point of denying black identity? What race could command respect of others without respecting its own values and culture? And who was to cherish those values and preserve that identity if not blacks themselves?

In two historic instances Negro Americans have been

beneficiaries—as well as the victims—of the national compulsion to level or to blur distinctions. The first leveling ended the legal status of slavery, the second the legal system of segregation. Both abolitions left the beneficiaries still suffering under handicaps inflicted by the system abolished. The emancipators made abortive and unsuccessful efforts to remove the handicaps and then proclaimed the emancipated equal. After the legal end of Jim Crow, the emancipated were expected to shed not only such distinctions as they abhorred but those distinctions they cherished as essential to their identity. They found they were unable to rid themselves fully of the former and unable wholly to abandon the latter. Under these circumstances the promise of integration took on a different aspect. So long as it had been truculently withheld, it had seemed infinitely more desirable than when it was grudgingly proffered at prices that seemed too high. Discontent could therefore continue to take both the form of a demand for integration and a demand for separation. Both demands would likely be heard for a long time, for the means of satisfying neither seemed yet at hand.

Notes on Reading

Among recent books dealing with historical aspects of race relations the following are of special interest: Richard C. Wade, *Slavery in the Cities: The South, 1820-1860* (1964); Leon F. Litwack, *North of Slavery: The Negro in the Free States, 1790-1860* (1961); and Joel Williamson, *After Slavery: The Negro in South Carolina During Reconstruction, 1861-1877* (1965). Two works on the period after Reconstruction have been of particular help: Charles E. Wynes, *Race Relations in Virginia, 1870-1902* (1961); and Frenise A. Logan, *The Negro in North Carolina, 1876-1894* (1964). A valuable history of racism is Thomas F. Gossett, *Race: The History of an Idea in America* (1964).

A most helpful synthesis of scholarship of its time is Gunnar Myrdal, *An American Dilemma: The Negro Problem and Modern Democracy* (2 vols., 1944). John

Hope Franklin, *From Slavery to Freedom: A History of Negro Americans* (1967) is the best-informed brief history of the subject. A critical period of American history is treated in C. Vann Woodward, *Origins of the New South, 1877-1913* (1951).

Old works of historic significance are W. E. B. DuBois, *The Souls of Black Folk* (1903); Arlin Turner (ed.), George W. Cable, *The Negro Question: A Selection of Writings on Civil Rights in the South* (1958); and a work originally published in 1889, C. Vann Woodward (ed.), Lewis H. Blair, *A Southern Prophecy: The Prosperity of the South Dependent upon the Elevation of the Negro* (1964).

Original investigations of importance on special subjects are Vernon L. Wharton, *The Negro in Mississippi, 1865-1890* (1947); George B. Tindall, *South Carolina Negroes, 1877-1900* (1952); and August Meier, *Negro Thought in America, 1880-1915* (1963). The desertion of Northern liberals is treated in Rayford W. Logan, *The Negro in American Life and Thought: The Nadir, 1877-1901* (1954). Legal aspects of race relations are examined in Pauli Murray, *State Laws on Race and Color* (1952); Albert P. Blaustein and Clarence C. Ferguson, Jr., *Desegregation and the Law* (1957); Charles S. Mangum, Jr., *The Legal Status of the Negro* (1940); Franklin Johnson, *The Development of State Legislation Concerning the Free Negro* (1919); Gilbert T. Stephenson, *Race Distinctions in American Law* (1910).

Of many sociological treatments, the following deserve particular attention: Thomas F. Pettigrew, *A*

Profile of the Negro American (1964); Gordon W. Allport, *The Nature of Prejudice* (1954); E. Franklin Frazier, *The Negro in the United States* (1949); Bertram W. Doyle, *The Etiquette of Race Relations in the South* (1937); and Arthur F. Raper, *The Tragedy of Lynching* (1933). Various works of John Dollard, particularly *Children of Bondage* (with Allison Davis, 1940), are illuminating. A most helpful essay is one by Guion G. Johnson, 'The Ideology of White Supremacy, 1876-1910,' in Fletcher Green, *Essays in Southern History* (1949).

Race factors in politics are astutely examined in V. O. Key, Jr., *Southern Politics in State and Nation* (1949). There is much of value in Paul Lewinson, *Race, Class, and Party, A History of Negro Suffrage and White Politics in the South* (1932), and William A. Mabry, *The Negro in North Carolina Politics since Reconstruction* (1940).

Useful accounts of the civil rights crusade in the South include Benjamin Muse, *Ten Years of Prelude: The Story of Integration since the Supreme Court's 1954 Decision* (1964), and the same author's *The American Negro Revolution: From Nonviolence to Black Power, 1963-1967* (1968): Anthony Lewis *et al., Portrait of a Decade: The Second American Revolution* (1964); Pat Watters, *Down to Now: Reflections on the Civil Rights Movement* (1971). On school desegregation see Gary Orfield, *The Reconstruction of Southern Education: The Schools and the 1964 Civil Rights Act* (1969); Charles E. Silberman, *Crisis in Black and White* (1964); and *Rev-*

olution in Civil Rights (1965), compiled by the Congressional Quarterly Service.

On the riots of 1965-68 several government-sponsored studies are the so-called Kerner Report, *Report of the National Advisory Commission on Civil Disorders* (1968) and *Supplemental Studies* (1968) of the same report; and two reports to The National Commission on the Causes and Prevention of Violence, one by Hugh Davis Graham and Ted Robert Gurr, *Violence in America: Historical and Comparative Perspectives* (2 vols., 1969); and another by Jerome H. Skolnick, *The Politics of Protest* (1969).

Black separatism and nationalism, and reactions to these movements are treated in August Meier and Elliott Rudwick, *CORE: A Study of the Civil Rights Movement, 1942-1948* (1973); John H. Bracey, Jr., August Meier, and Elliot Rudwick, eds., *Black Nationalism in America* ((1970) ; Theodore Draper, *The Rediscovery of Black Nationalism* (1970); Thomas R. Dye, *The Politics of Equality* (1971); Bayard Rustin, *Down the Line: Collected Writings* (1971); and William H. Grier and Price M. Cobbs, *Black Rage* (1968).

Index